THE COUGAR ALMANAC

Books by Robert H. Busch

Wolf Songs

The Wolf Almanac

Gray Whales, Wandering Giants

Valley of the Grizzlies

Salmon Country

On Otter Pond

Loons

THE COUGAR ALMANAC

A COMPLETE NATURAL HISTORY OF THE MOUNTAIN LION

ROBERT H. BUSCH

THE LYONS PRESS
Guilford, Connecticut
An imprint of The Globe Pequot Press

The Lyons Press is an imprint of The Globe Pequot Press.

10 9 8 7 6 5 4 3 2 1

Printed in the United States of America

ISBN 1-59228-295-4

The Library of Congress has cataloged a hardcover edition as follows:

Busch, Robert.
    The cougar almanac : a complete natural history of the mountain lion / Robert H. Busch.
        p. cm.
    Includes bibliographical references and index.
    ISBN 1-55821-403-8
    1. Pumas I. Title.

QL737.C23B88 1996
599.74'528—dc20   96-22399
                                                        CIP

For Luke and Kato, missed and loved.

CONTENTS

Acknowledgments

Thanks are due to the numerous individuals who assisted in the compilation of this book: Knut Atkinson, British Columbia Wildlife Branch; Marion Baker-Gierlach, Wildlife Damage Review; Dee Seton Barber, Ernest Thompson Seton Institute, Inc.; John Gunson, Alberta Fish and Wildlife Division; Lyn Hancock; Martin Jalkotzy, Arc Associated Resource Consultants; Don Jackson, Turpentine Exotic Wildlife Ranch; Dennis Jordan, U.S. Fish and Wildlife Service; James Laray, Everglades National Park; Doug Moreschi, Friends of the Everglades; Dan Lay; Jeff Morgan; Ted Reed, Friends of the Eastern Panther; and the dedicated staffs of the Canadian Wildlife Service, Colorado Division of Wildlife, Glacier National Park, State of New Mexico Department of Game and Fish, and Texas Parks and Wildlife Department.

And to my editor, Lilly Golden, my thanks for sometimes making gems out of gravel.

PREFACE

Autumn had thrown its golden cloak over the land, and the earth lay hushed. The eerie howls of hounds pierced the icy air. After a one-hour dash through devil's club and over deadfalls they had finally treed their target. High above the hounds, draped like a plush rug over the twisted limbs of an elderly ponderosa pine, was a cougar.

A half mile back, two of us scrambled over the thick brush. Biologist Mike Atkinson carried a large pack full of veterinary equipment. He looked like a doctor making an extremely distant house call. I stumbled behind, one hand clutching a notebook, the other my heart. *I gotta get more exercise* ran like a mantra through my mind. Finally, we reached the wind-whipped pine in which our prey was perched. The cougar felt secure in his tree and showed no fear. Cougars in similar situations—held at bay by curious humans below—have even fallen asleep.

Mike studied the big cat through binoculars to estimate his weight and then fired a tranquilizer dart into his hip. The cougar hissed at this gross invasion of his privacy, then slowly nodded off. Donning climbing gear, Mike clambered up the tree and gently pulled the cat to earth. A half-dozen measurements were quickly taken:

total length: 6′3″	height to shoulder: 26″
tail length: 2′4″	weight: 84 lbs.

The cat was thin for his age; the winter had been hard. He was injected with vitamins and a dewormer, and an antibiotic was applied to a deep cut on one shoulder. A small blood sample was taken. While Mike attended to his medical needs, I stared at the beautiful animal lying at my feet. His fur was coarse and thick, and even in repose, the musculature was evident. But it was the big cat's eyes that impressed me so—great amber orbs set like gems in a massive head. After the cat was plotted and prodded, weighed and wired with a radio transmitter, we moved him into the shade to recover.

As I quickly scribbled additional notes, the cat staggered to his feet. When I looked up, he was gone.

The radio transmitter is working still, giving biologists data on the cougar's travels through the dense brush of central British Columbia. A lot remains to be learned: Why do cougars here seem to be less aggressive than their cousins on Vancouver Island? How is their prey base holding up? How are the cougars interacting with the resident wolf packs? And what is their future, given the ever-increasing human population in the area?

That was my first trip into cougar country. My memories of the chase, which left me with branch-ripped jeans and gashed arms, are fading. I don't recall the campfire meals, only that they were usually either half burned or half raw. I've tried to forget the afternoon that I fell into an icy creek and gave out a yell that scared off every cougar within a hundred miles. But I will always remember those eyes.

That treed cougar was the second I've seen in the wild. I'm lucky—that's two more than most people will ever see.

I spotted the first animal four years ago, when I lived in the foothills of southern Alberta. Early one morning, an adult cougar stepped up from a ditch and crossed the road right in front of my car. It was beautiful. The headlights spotlighted the gloss of its coat, and the amber eyes shone like wave-polished pebbles. The cougar stared at my vehicle for a few seconds, then calmly strolled across the road. Even though the grass beside the road was parched and crackled underfoot, the big cat made no sound as it slipped away into an island of trees. The perfect predator.

A few weeks later, I was talking to a neighbor, a rancher who lived a few miles down the road. I mentioned seeing the cougar, and received an aggressive grunt in reply. "We had one of those things on the ranch last year," he said. I asked what had happened to it. "Shot it," he snapped. "You don't want those things hanging around." I could have replied that I didn't want neighbors like him around either, but I bit my tongue.

None of his livestock had been touched, and no damage was done to his property or family, but he had taken the cougar's life just because it was a cougar, a predator, an animal that kills other animals in order to survive.

It's because of attitudes like that of my rancher neighbor that predators across North America have shown alarming declines. In most parts of America, the wolf was long gone by the 1920s. In all but the wildest corners, the grizzly was exterminated by the 1960s. Across the bulk of the continent, the only major predator left is the cougar. However, its habitat is disappearing fast, and its popularity as the last of the big-game trophy predators is growing.

It has survived because of its intelligence, its agility, and its elusive nature. It has been an animal of mystery until only recently. Almost all of what we now know about the cougar we've learned in the past twenty years. And with that knowledge comes hope— hope that if the cougar has made it this far, it will continue to do so.

I now live in the Cariboo country of central British Columbia, where a neighbor spotted a female cougar and two young ones strolling through her woods not long ago. The news made me smile. There are still some left. They've still got a chance. It's not too late.

I wish them luck.

Robert H. Busch
Fall 1996

THE
CAT
OF GOD

▼▼▼

COUGAR EVOLUTION, RANGE, AND HABITAT

➤ COMMON NAMES
➤ FOR THE COUGAR

W hile researching this book, I requested information on cougars from a state wildlife branch. "Oh," the receptionist replied. "We have nothing on cougars, but we do have data on pumas we can send you." Both terms, of course, refer to the same animal.

When Christopher Columbus skirted the shores of North America in 1502, he spotted what he called "leones," or lions. Today, the cougar is known by a myriad of monickers, including mountain lion, catamount (cat-of-the-mountain), ghost cat, king cat, devil cat, Indian devil, deer tiger, yellow tiger, red tiger, panther, painter (a corruption of panther), and screamer. One eager researcher uncovered over three dozen other names in the English language alone. The two most common are cougar and puma.

The word *cougar* is an amalgam of two Native Brazilian words for the jaguar: the Tupi word *cuacuara,* and the similar Guarani word *guacuara.* When the eighteenth-century French naturalist Comte George-Louis Leclerc de Buffon wrote his mammoth *Histoire Naturelle,* he melded these two words into the word *cuguar,* which was then distorted again into its current spelling. (Buffon was equally inaccurate in his math: He once calculated that all life on Earth had begun about forty thousand years ago. He was off by about four billion years.)

Puma is a Peruvian Quechua Indian word meaning "a powerful animal." It was absorbed unchanged into the Spanish language by the Natives' conquerors, and then into English. The word first appeared in print in 1783.

In South America they call the great cat *Amigo del Christiano,* "Friend of Christian," a tribute to the gentle and friendly nature of the beast. Early French Canadians called the cougar *carcajou,* a name later given to the wolverine, causing much confusion among early biologists. To the Cherokee, the cougar was *Klandaghi,* "Lord of the Forest." The Cree called it *Katalgar,* "Greatest of Wild Hunters." Puget Sound Natives called it the Fire Cat, believing that, in the fall of each year, the great cat carried fire from the Olympic Mountains to Mount Rainier, starting a forest fire along the way. New Brunswick's Malecite Natives called the cougar *Pi-twal,* the "Long-Tailed One." The Chickasaw called it *Ko-Icto,* the "Cat of God."

EVOLUTION

Tucked among the posh shops on Wilshire Boulevard in Los Angeles is the George C. Page Museum. Here the visitor can stroll among models of some of the earliest cats in North America, including the famed saber-toothed tiger, an early cousin of today's cougar.

Scientists know the cougar as *Felis concolor* ("cat of one color"), a name bestowed by Carolus Linnaeus in 1771. The Felid family first evolved in the Eocene or Lower Oligocene epoch, about forty million years ago. Their ancestor was a beast known as *Dinictis,* a lynx-sized cat that evolved into two branches: the large, clumsy, saber-toothed Nimravids and the smaller, faster Felids.

The saber-toothed cats are known through fossil records to have evolved about ten genera. The best known is *Smilodon,* a lion-sized cat that sported huge canine teeth about 6 inches long. *Smilodon* is the saber-tooth found by the hundreds in the famous La Brea tar pits in Los Angeles. With oversized canines and an undersized brain, it and all the other saber-tooths soon traveled down the one-way road to extinction. By ten thousand years ago, the last saber-tooth had disappeared from North America. (It's interesting that the canine family saw a parallel type of evolutionary success: The large and slow dire wolf died out over seven thousand years ago, but the smaller and more agile modern wolf has survived.)

The Felids have proved to be one of the most successful of animal families, with thirty-five species populating all of the continents except Australia. One measure of their success is the fact that cat anatomy has survived almost unchanged for over ten million years; most other mammals underwent drastic evolutionary changes during that time. Although the fossil record of Felids is incomplete, the basic sequence of cat evolution is well known.

About ten to twenty million years ago, the Felids began branching into a number of cat genera. One genus, *Leo,* formerly called *Panthera,* includes the roaring cats: lions, tigers, leopards, snow

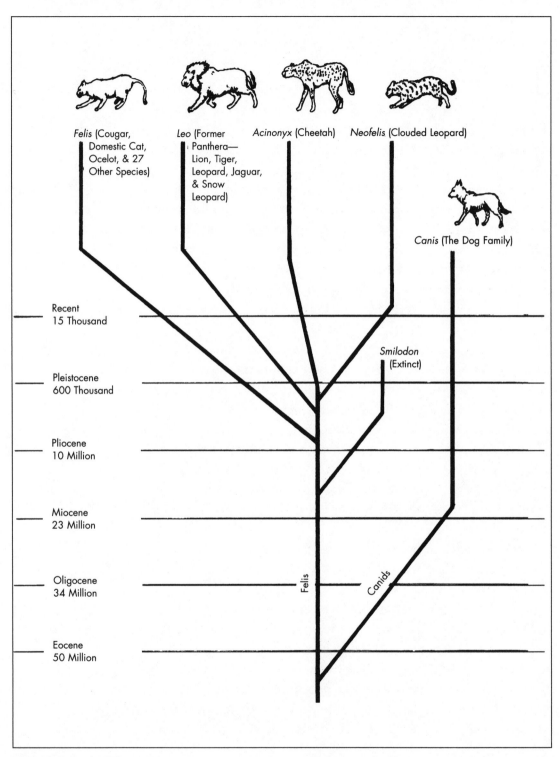

Felis (Cougar, Domestic Cat, Ocelot, & 27 Other Species)

Leo (Former Panthera—Lion, Tiger, Leopard, Jaguar, & Snow Leopard)

Acinonyx (Cheetah)

Neofelis (Clouded Leopard)

Canis (The Dog Family)

Recent 15 Thousand

Pleistocene 600 Thousand

Smilodon (Extinct)

Pliocene 10 Million

Miocene 23 Million

Oligocene 34 Million

Felis

Canids

Eocene 50 Million

COUGAR FAMILY TREE

leopards, and jaguars. The genus *Felis* includes the domestic cat and the small wild cats, including the lynx, bobcat, sand cat, fishing cat, cougar, and over two dozen others. The smallest *Felis* is the tiny rusty-spotted cat of India and Sri Lanka, which weighs barely 3 pounds. The largest *Felis* is the cougar. The reason for the classification lies in the cougar's anatomy.

All of the small cats have a solid hyoid, or tongue bone, at the base of their tongues. The hyoid is attached to the muscles of both the windpipe and the larynx. The roaring cats, on the other hand, have a flexible cartilage at the base of their tongues, which creates the vibrating sound that we call a roar. The cougar, like its smaller cousins in the *Felis* genus, has a solid hyoid and therefore doesn't roar.

Hybrid crosses of captive cougar-leopards, cougar-tigers, and cougar-jaguars demonstrate the close genetic affiliations among the whole cat family.

The cheetah is probably the most recently evolved wild Felid, currently classed in a genus of its own, *Acynonyx*. Many people have pointed out that the cheetah and the cougar have much in common, and perhaps shared a common ancestor. Biologist D. B. Adams once wrote that cougars and cheetahs "may be more closely related to each other than either is to any other living cat." Neither cat can roar, but both can purr. The chirps, cheeps, and whistles emitted by both cats are similar. Both have round pupils that don't form slits, whereas all *Felis* members, but the cougar, have pupils that do. Both have extralong hind legs and long, streaming tails. And the reproductive physiology of both cats is strikingly similar.

It's also interesting that up to a few tens of thousands of years ago, there were cheetahs in North America. Some biologists believe that they left the continent via the Bering land bridge and then spread to Asia and Africa, leaving behind the cougar to occupy the same basic ecological niche.

If this is true, why didn't the cougars cross the bridge as well? Some have suggested that the reason was food. The cougar hunts by stealth, and would have had a hard time concealing itself on the

Cougar (*Felis concolor*) Subspecies

NORTH AMERICA

F. c. couguar—Eastern cougar	browni—Yuma puma
schorgeri—Wisconsin cougar	improcera—Baja California cougar
missoulensis—Missoula cougar	azteca—Mexican cougar
hippolestes—Colorado cougar	stanleyana—Texas cougar
oregonensis—Oregon cougar	coryi—Florida panther
vancouverensis—Vancouver Island cougar	mayensis—Mayan cougar
californica—California cougar	costaricensis—Costa Rican puma
kaibabensis—Kaibab cougar	

SOUTH AMERICA

F. c. concolor—Brazilian cougar	acrocodia—Mato Grosso cougar
bangsi—Colombian cougar	puma—Chilean puma
söderströmi—Ecuador cougar	cabrerae—Argentine puma
discolor—Amazon cougar	pearsoni—Pearson's puma
incarum—Incan cougar	patagonica—Patagonia puma
osgoodi—Bolivian cougar	araucanus—Andes puma

treeless tundra that exists in the empty northern stretches of North America. The cheetah, however, is a long-distance chaser, a creature of treeless plains, and would have had no problem running down its food on the tundra.

The first cougar in North America appeared during the Upper Pliocene epoch, about two million years ago. During the following Pleistocene epoch, there were a number of cougar species, but of them all only *Felis concolor* survives today. It may have appeared as early as one and a half million years ago. Biologists believe that the cougar first crossed the Panama land bridge into South America about one million years ago.

Best known of all Felids, of course, is the ubiquitous house cat. The common house cat (*Felis catus*) was domesticated somewhere between thirty-five hundred and seven thousand years ago in the Mediterranean area, the descendant of a small prehistoric feline that first appeared in Africa. Actually, we didn't domesticate the house cat; more accurately, it adopted us. After humans learned to harvest grain, rodents began to move in after it, and cats moved in after the rodents. To contemporary owners of independent house cats, the fact that the cats made the first move comes as no surprise.

➤RANGE

A few years ago, when in Mexico, I asked about the local cougar population. A local rancher, who had lived in the country for over a decade, replied that there were no cougars in Mexico, and never had been. The man was wrong, but his lack of knowledge about cougars is typical. Because most people have never seen one, they assume that in their area the cats simply don't exist.

Originally, the cougar had the most widespread range of any wild American mammal. It could once be found from the southern tip of Chile right up to northern British Columbia; from east to west, its range crossed the entire girth of both North and South America. Occasionally, the big cat strayed north into Alaska or the Yukon. In 1989, one was shot near Wrangell in southern Alaska. In North America, the cougar never reached the Queen Charlotte Islands off the West Coast and never populated either Prince Edward Island or Newfoundland on the East Coast.

Today, the cougar is found in British Columbia and Alberta in Canada, in the twelve westernmost states (California, Oregon, Washington, Idaho, Montana, Utah, Nevada, New Mexico, Arizona, Colorado, Texas, and Wyoming) and in Florida. Occasionally, the animals stray outside of these areas: Reliable reports place cougars in the southern Yukon and in Alberta–Northwest Territories border areas in the 1960s and early 1970s, and one was shot near Cutknife, Saskatchewan, in 1975. Many of these strays are

found along major river valleys, which act as transportation corridors for both cougars and prey. In Central and South America, the cougar may be found in scattered locations from Mexico to Chile.

HABITAT

The lofty mountains of Peru are probably the last places most people would expect to see cougars, but many varied habitats, including deserts, forests, mountains, and lowlands, were all home to the early cats. But then came humans. Today, the cougar has been pushed to the attics of the New World, to the mountains, ridges, deserts, and swamps where people seldom stray. Just imagine an environment in which you wouldn't want to build a house: the high rocky ridges of Montana, the soggy swamps of Florida, the dusty deserts of Arizona. These are the places where we've pushed the cougar. In the United States, the cougar is now absent from almost two-thirds of its previous range. This is its last stand.

Generally, the cougar prefers habitat that provides good forage for its prey and enough cover for it to efficiently stalk that prey. In Idaho, for example, researchers have found that the big cats prefer steep, rugged areas with good fir and pine cover. They've noted that the cougars avoid open areas, tending to keep to borders where the woods provide cover. The availability of cover seems to be more important than the type of vegetation in the area. In Wyoming, cougars showed a similar preference for steep terrain with mixed, wooded cover. The two most highly used zones in the Wyoming study were streamside areas and rock ledges. In central British Columbia, cougars are rarely found in the valley bottoms; usually, they only appear in the wooded highlands. In Arizona, it was found that some cougars starved rather than follow deer into lower elevations and unfamiliar habitat.

The cougar has a high tolerance for heat, and is quite at ease in the parched lowlands of North America. In fact, two of the largest cougars ever recorded came from, respectively, the arid Okanagan Lake area of southern British Columbia, and the scorched drylands of Utah.

Where the territories of the cougar overlap those of the other big American cat, the jaguar, in Central and South America, the cougar has shown a distinct preference for drier areas. In the Pantanal area of Brazil's Mato Grosso state, biologist George Schaller found that the jaguar preferred wet lowlands, and the cougar the drier portions of range. In Belize, American biologist Alan Rabinowitz reported that cougars again preferred the high, dry ridges and left the moist lowlands to the jaguar.

Altitude hardly seems to bother the hardy cat, for it has been spotted at fifteen thousand feet roaming among the lofty crags of the Andes in South America.

Cougar Populations

The elusive nature of the cougar makes it a difficult animal to census. In fact, Colorado biologist Allen E. Anderson once stated that "of all large North American game animals, puma are perhaps the least amenable to census." Population estimates for North American cougars range from ten to fifty thousand. Whatever the actual number, for a major predator it's quite low. (Compare this with the bobcat, for example, which numbers over one million in the United States alone.)

The highest cougar population in Canada is in British Columbia, which more than six thousand cats call home. In the United States, the highest number is probably in California, with three to five thousand cougars. Parts of California have a cougar population density as high as 1 cat per 10 square miles.

E. A. Goldman reported in 1946 that cougars had been common throughout Mexico in the early 1900s. However, by 1959, A. S. Leopold stated in his book *Wildlife of Mexico* that they were "scarce or exterminated locally in settled areas." In South America, Goldman thought that "Patagonia probably contains more pumas than are to be found in any other part of South America." Naturalist Anne La Bastille reported in 1973 that the cougar population in Panama was already small and decreasing. C. B. Koford found in 1976 that cougars were rare in El Salvador. There are no current population estimates for cougars in Mexico, or in Central or South America. In these areas, the elusive Cat of God remains uncounted.

THE
BIG
CAT

▼▼▼

COUGAR ANATOMY
AND PHYSIOLOGY

PHYSICAL DESCRIPTION

That first time I spotted a wild cougar, it disappeared into the woods in a matter of seconds. But my main memory years later is of a long streaming tail visible long after the body of the animal was engulfed in brush. It was as if the cougar were waving good-bye.

Adult cougars stand about 30 inches high at the shoulder and

may stretch over 8 feet from nose to tail. The thick, ropelike tail is often about a third of the total body length, and provides balance during the animal's mighty leaps. Both of the other two common wild American cats, the lynx and the bobcat, have short, stubby tails—an important distinction for field identification.

The cougar's tail has generated more myths than any other part of its anatomy. Contrary to common folklore, the cougar does not lash its tail from side to side to show its wrath. It does not twitch the tip of its tail to attract inquisitive prey. And the tail is not carried curled up and pointed to the left side, as was claimed by one early zoologist. In 1770, Thomas Jeffreys even wrote that the cougar's tail is "so long as to wrap several times around his body." Not even close.

The heaviest cougar on record is a 276-pound male shot near Hillsdale, Arizona, in 1917. This huge animal measured 8 feet, 7¾ inches long. The heaviest cougar documented in recent times was a 227-pound cat shot in Montana in 1970. There's also a record of a captive cougar in Idaho that weighed 220 pounds.

Cougars in excess of 200 pounds are quite rare; most are in the 75- to 175-pound range, with adult males weighing about 60 percent more than adult females. Although these are respectable figures, the cougar is still a bantamweight among wild cats: The heaviest tiger on record weighed a hefty 932 pounds, and the heaviest known lion, 690.

Ernest Thompson Seton once described the cougar as the perfect example of "lithe and splendid beasthood." Whereas the other big American cat, the jaguar, is short and squat, the cougar is long and lanky. In rare squabbles between the two big cats, Central American Natives report that the cougar's speed and agility often give it the upper hand, although the jaguar is much stronger, and usually heavier.

Despite its speed and agility, the cougar tires quickly. Its heartbeat is twice as rapid as a human's, and a short period of exertion exhausts the animal. It's a sprinter, not a long-distance chaser.

Although most cougars are a tawny brown color, shades of apricot, rust, lemon, and smoke have been recorded. Theodore Roosevelt, who shot fourteen cougars on a single hunting trip in Colorado in 1901, once wrote that even though all the cats were shot in the same general area, "some were slate gray…others rufous." (One of the cougars shot by Roosevelt on this trip held the position of third-largest cougar ever shot in North America in Boone and Crockett Club records for many years. The animal was 8 feet long and weighed 227 pounds. It's now preserved in the U.S. National Museum in Washington.) The throat and underparts of a cougar are usually white, and the tail is tipped with black.

There have been a number of reports of black cougars, especially from Central America. In North America, too, black cougars have been reported in Texas, and one was reputedly spotted several years ago north of Okanagan Lake in British Columbia. An intriguing report also came out of the Cariboo Lake area of central British Columbia, where a small black cougar with spots still visible was seen by two reliable witnesses. (Young cougars are spotted and lose their spots with age.)

However, in the southern United States, both the jaguar and its smaller cousin, the jaguarundi, have dark gray color phases; these may have led to mistakenly identified black cougars. In addition, the knowledge of black panthers' existence in Africa may have influenced more than one of these reports. (Despite the number of black panther tales originating from Africa, the black panther is not a panther at all, but a rare, black color phase of the common leopard.) Albino cougars have been reported, but have never been documented in any collection of live animals or skins.

To hide from pursuers, a cougar often merely crouches low in deep grass or remains motionless on a rocky perch. The neutral color of the cat blends in effectively with a variety of backgrounds. Recently, the editors of *Natural History* magazine apologized in an article on cougars; they stated that "cougars are so adept at concealment that they are almost impossible to photograph in the wild." Most of the photos accompanying the article, and indeed most published photos of cougars, were of captive cougars in a game farm setting.

Cougar fur is short and coarse compared to the longer, silky coats of other felines such as the lynx and tiger. Therefore, it's rarely used in clothing, and then only as trim on parkas or hats. The cougar is one of the two large cats that does not sport a spotted or striped coat. (The lion is the other.) This simple fact has been a crucial factor in saving the cougar from the trapping pressures felt by other wild cats. The cougar is indeed dressed for success.

The hide of a cougar is quite loose: to some people, it looks like it's wearing a coat one size too large. But in fights with other predators, a roomy hide allows injuries to remain superficial and not harm the more important internal organs.

Unlike its African cousin, the lion, the male mountain lion does not have a mane. This led to a great deal of confusion on the part of early fur traders. In New York, Dutch traders assumed that all the cougar skins they were sent were those of females, as none of the hides had manes. They asked Native American hunters for the

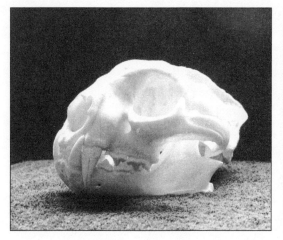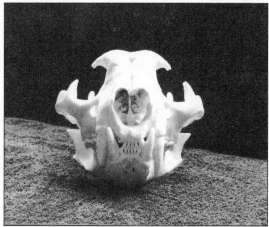

explanation, and the latter told the traders that the males hid out in remote mountainous places and could not be hunted.

Male cougars, like all male cats, are known as toms. The term originated in an anonymous story published in 1760 entitled "The Life and Adventures of a Cat." The male cat in the story was called Tom the Cat, and the name has stuck.

Cougars have short, blunt snouts concealing powerful jaws. Their jaws are heavily boned to absorb the shock of struggling prey. Cougars don't have large molars for chewing; instead, their teeth are adapted for tearing and biting. Unlike humans, cougars don't use their front incisors for cutting through small bits of food. Instead, the third molars on both the lower and upper jaw are modified into sharp blades called carnassials, which are used to slice flesh. Most of the other teeth are small and of little use; most of the side teeth don't meet when the cougar's mouth is closed. The large canine teeth, however, are used to stab and hold prey and may be over 1½ inches long. When a young female cougar was accidentally cornered in a barn in central British Columbia, it was the animal's fangs that impressed the barn's owner the most: "It had a beautiful coat, all right, but I'll sure never forget those teeth."

The cougar's ears are relatively short and rounded and signal the cat's moods. Ears that are perked straight up signal a cat that is attentive or pleased. Ears flattened against the head tell knowledgeable hikers to back off.

The long whiskers on either side of the muzzle are linked to nerve connections that transmit information about items contacted. They're used both for tactile sensing and to help the cat find its way in the dark, by means of detecting air currents flowing around objects in a cat's path. In other cats, it has also been shown that whiskers aid in detecting when prey has stopped struggling. House cats, for example, will wrap their whiskers around a mouse to transmit information on the prey's last movements. The tip of the nose, the toes, and the paws are all very sensitive to touch, as well.

Seen close up, cougars seem to have the shoulders of a linebacker, piles of muscle that can launch the animal into incredible leaps. Horizontal bounds of twenty feet and vertical jumps of sixteen feet have been documented by field biologists. Stanley Young, in *The Puma: Mysterious American Cat,* recorded a downward leap of sixty feet. However, campfire tales of cougars leaping ten-foot fences clutching calves in their jaws are pure fiction.

One California observer, however, has seen a cougar "jump downward, and then, while in midair, turn almost sixty degrees to one side, so as to make a landing the animal could not have seen when he leaped." Their fluid agility is amazing.

THE IMPRESSIVE CANINES OF AN ADULT COUGAR
(© ERWIN & PEGGY BAUER)

||||

SENSES

A cougar's eyes are quite large relative to those of other mammals. They provide a wide angle of vision, up to 285 degrees, which aids the cat in sighting prey (humans can only see through a 210-degree angle). The retina of the cougar's eye has more rods than cones, a sign of excellent night vision (we humans have more cones than rods and thus can literally not see our hands in front of us in near-darkness). Behind the cougar's retina is a mirrorlike layer called the *tapetum lucidum* (Latin for "bright carpet"), which amplifies dim light. The result is that they require only one-sixth as much light as humans to discern details at night. Contrary to myth, neither the cougar nor any other cat can see in total darkness.

Cougars are thought to have some degree of color vision, but this has not been adequately tested. (Domestic cats can distinguish between red and green, red and blue, red and gray, green and blue, green and gray, blue and gray, yellow and blue, and yellow and gray.)

Their sense of hearing is vastly superior to that of humans, picking up ultrasonic sounds far beyond the human range. This ability to hear high frequencies may aid the cat in detecting high-pitched mouse vocalizations even when the tiny prey is hidden under leaves or snow.

Although the cougar's sense of smell is thought to be about thirty times better than that of humans, it's not well developed compared to that of other wild animals. It's believed to be much less important to a hunting cougar than sight or hearing. One Colorado researcher buried fresh meat under six inches of packed snow and watched to see if a captive cougar could detect it. "He walked right over that spot for half an hour and never smelled a thing," the biologist wrote.

A cougar's sense of taste is quite limited: Its tongue has less than five hundred taste buds, compared with the human's nine thousand, giving the cat a decreased ability to detect a wide range of tastes. Unlike wild Canids, the cougar has no taste receptors for sweetness on its tongue, so such treats as sweet berries are rarely on its menu; its diet is generally restricted to mammal and bird flesh. Even the cat's digestive system is geared for a purely meat diet. Meat is relatively easy to digest, so the cougar's intestine is short, allowing for quick absorption of nutrients.

A YOUNG COUGAR LEAVES ITS MOTHER
BETWEEN THE AGES OF NINE MONTHS
AND TWENTY-FOUR MONTHS.

ADULT COUGAR TRACKS ARE
THREE INCHES LONG AND
USUALLY DO NOT SHOW
CLAW MARKS.

||||

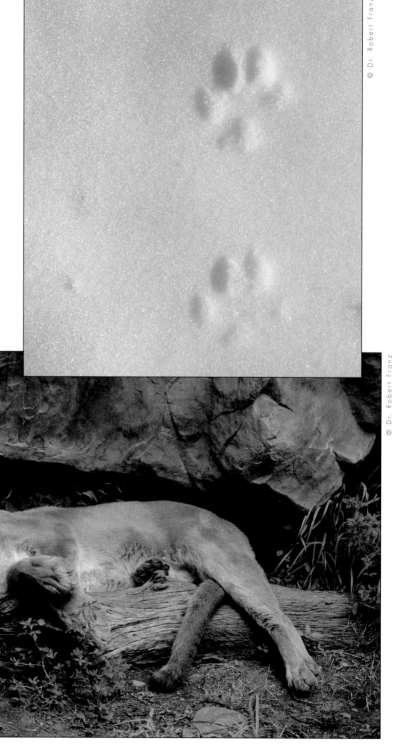

COUGARS MAY SLEEP FOR SIXTEEN
HOURS PER DAY AND ONLY EAT
ONCE EVERY TWO TO THREE WEEKS.

||||

A COUGAR'S ROUGH TONGUE
CAN LICK THE FUR OFF PREY OR
CLEAN A DIRTY PAW.

\\\\

A YOUNG COUGAR KITTEN
EXPLORING THE BIG WILD WORLD.

\\\\

COUGAR KITTENS CAN
CLIMB TREES BY THE AGE
OF THREE MONTHS.

\\\\

THE SHARP EYESIGHT OF THE
COUGAR IS CRUCIAL TO ITS
HUNTING SUCCESS.

\\\\

UNLIKE MANY CATS, COUGARS
READILY TAKE TO WATER.

\|\|\|

THE NIGHT VISION OF A COUGAR IS
SIX TIMES THAT OF A HUMAN.

\\\\

COUGARS CAN BE FOUND IN A VARIETY
OF HABITATS, FROM SEA-LEVEL DESERTS
TO 15,000-FOOT MOUNTAINS.

||||

THE TAWNY COLORATION OF THE COUGAR
PROVIDES EXCELLENT CAMOUFLAGE.

||||

THE DISTINCTIVE SNARL OF
AN ANGRY COUGAR.

\\\\

A FEMALE COUGAR TESTS THE
AIR FOR SCENTS.

\\\\

THE FEMALE COUGAR IS AN
ATTENTIVE MOTHER.

||||

THE COUGAR IS TWO-TONE:
TAWNY ABOVE AND WHITE BELOW.

||||

TWO CAPTIVE JUVENILE
COUGARS SLEEPING
SIDE BY SIDE.

||||

© Lyn Hancock

© Erwin & Peggy Bauer

A COUGAR CHASING PREY
CAN EXCEED SPEEDS OF 45 MPH.

||||

THE GORY BUSINESS
OF FEEDING UPON
A FRESH KILL.
\|\|\|\|

© William E. Rideg

© Knut Atkinson

A TYPICAL DEER KILL, WITH AN OPENING
INTO THE SIDE OF THE BODY AND THE
INTERNAL ORGANS EATEN FIRST.
\|\|\|\|

THE ALERT ATTITUDE OF A YOUNG COUGAR:
EARS UPRIGHT, EYES FOCUSED,
AND BODY LOW TO THE GROUND.

THE MUSCULAR
HINDQUARTERS OF THE
COUGAR POWER THE
ANIMAL'S MIGHTY LEAPS.
\\\\

© Erwin & Peggy Bauer

Dennis Jordan, U.S. Fish & Wildlife Service

A RARE PHOTO OF
THE ELUSIVE FLORIDA PANTHER.
\\\\

ONE OF THE PRIME WINTER FOODS FOR THE
COUGAR IS THE SNOWSHOE HARE.

||||

COUGARS OFTEN TAKE TO THE TREES
TO ESCAPE PURSUERS.

The cougar's tongue is covered with rough papillae, useful in self-grooming and in licking the fur off prey.

Cats of all kinds possess another sensory organ absent in humans. In the roof of cats' mouths, just behind the upper front teeth, is a little tube opening. This is the Jacobsen's organ, also known as the vomero-nasal organ. It's very sensitive to airborne chemicals and is used primarily by males to detect female sex hor-

THE FLEHMEN GESTURE IS PRIMARILY USED BY MALE COUGARS TO DETECT AIRBORNE FEMALE HORMONES.
(© THOMAS KITCHIN)

mones. In order to use the organ, the cat opens its mouth slightly, tilts back its head, wrinkles up its nose, and closes its eyes. Although it looks like the cat is responding to a particularly repulsive smell, it's in fact doing quite the opposite. This curious grimace is called the *flehmen* gesture or response.

SCAT AND TRACKS

Cougar scat is large compared with almost any other scat you might find in the woods. It may be as large as 9½ inches long and 1¼ inches in diameter.

THE LARGE FEET OF THE COUGAR ACT AS EFFICIENT SNOWSHOES IN WINTER.

(© ERWIN & PEGGY BAUER)

Cougars have oversized paws that act as big furry snowshoes in deep powder snow. The leathery footpads muffle the big cat's approaches to prey, and between the pads are sweat glands that help dissipate excess heat. Cougars can also cool off by changing their skin's surface temperature and by decreasing blood flow to their limbs.

Adult cougar tracks are about 3½ inches wide by 3 inches long. Although in the 1940s biologist Stanley Young recorded seeing a cougar track almost 7 inches wide, it's likely that this track was impressed into a soft substratum that distorted its size. During the research for this book, I was repeatedly confronted by hunters and guides who insisted that cougar tracks are huge. "Jeez, these things were five, six inches across," one told me. But when I found the tracks myself and measured them, they barely exceeded 3 inches. As is the case with most predators, much of what is "known" about the cougar is overestimated. If an animal looms large in our minds, so must its tracks, weight, and height.

One way to distinguish cougar tracks from small wolf tracks or large coyote tracks is to note the lack of claw marks in front of the toe pads. Cougars have retractile claws, but Canids do not. The retraction is achieved by an intricate mechanism involving two tendons attached to opposite sides of the claw bone. The movement that unsheaths the claws also spreads the toes, improving the efficiency of the grip. All species of cat, except the cheetah, have this unique mechanism.

A cougar's front pawprints are slightly larger than those of its back feet. Each track consists of four toe-pad prints and a "heel," or metacarpal pad, print. The front foot actually has five toes, but the "thumb" is elevated and does not show up in tracks. (Cougars, like all cats, actually walk on their toes, with their heels in the air. Biologists call this digitigrade motion. Humans use plantigrade motion, walking on their heels and the flats of their feet.)

Lynx prints look very similar to those of the cougar, but are slightly smaller. Cougar prints have a scalloped heel print while lynx prints don't. Bobcat prints are much smaller, rarely exceeding 2 inches in length.

In areas where the jaguar and cougar coexist, their tracks can be distinguished by the cougar's longer and more elliptical toe prints and more deeply scalloped heel prints. Jaguar tracks also tend to be more circular in general outline.

Depending on the speed at which the animal is traveling, the distance between cougar tracks ranges from 20 to 32 inches. The straddle, or distance between left and right pawprints, is about 8 to 10 inches. If the animal is moving rapidly, the hind paws may overstep the front paws by about 7 inches.

During the winter, the tail of the cougar may drag in deep snow and leave a rut running between the pawprints. Cougars will often place their hind feet into their forepaw prints in deep snow—to save energy, and perhaps to confuse pursuers as well. Cougars will also preferentially take the hard-packed sections of dirt trails in order to leave fewer prints. They've been known to deliberately circumvent patches of snow, either to avoid leaving tracks or to prevent getting their feet wet.

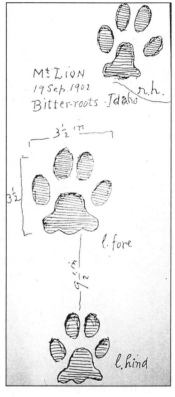

A 1902 SKETCH OF
COUGAR TRACKS
FOUND IN IDAHO BY
ERNEST THOMPSON
SETON

⋮ Diseases and Mortality

Life during winter can be hard on a cougar and many fail to find sufficient food to survive. In the winter of 1993, an emaciated female cougar grabbed a dog from an acreage near the shore of Quesnel Lake in central British Columbia. The next week, it came back for the other dog on the property and was shot. Many such cases occur during periods of deep snow and limited food. One unfortunate juvenile cougar in the United States was recently found dead with nothing but the wing cases of a beetle in its stomach.

Severe temperatures are also a problem in the winter. Alberta cougar researcher Ian Ross has reported that "many cougars that we captured had bobbed tails or shortened ears, probably the result of early cases of frostbite."

Other hazards facing the cougar include a whole host of internal and external parasites, including *Trichinella* worms, hookworms, tapeworms, roundworms, botflies, lice, ticks, and lung flukes.

In one study of cougars in southern Alberta, one in three had porcupine quills embedded in its flesh. Normally, these quills don't cause the cat any great harm, although an adult cougar in Colorado was found to have starved to death in 1977 after quills in its tongue prevented it from eating. Cougars may also die if quills puncture their stomach wall and pierce the abdominal cavity. Most quills either eventually fall out or dissolve.

I once came across a porcupine carcass in the foothills of southern Alberta that had been neatly sliced open from beneath and gutted. "Cougar," my neighbor told me. "Nothing else can kill a porcupine like that." Like almost everything else he believed about animals, he was wrong. In fact, fishers, wolves, and bears have all mastered the technique of flipping a porcupine onto its back and eating the underparts.

In 1970, it was discovered that some cougars in California were infected with feline panleukopenia, a viral disease they probably caught from domestic cats. Symptoms of the disease include vomiting, diarrhea, blood in the feces, and severe dehydration. In domestic kittens, it has a 90 percent mortality rate. Its affect on wild mortality is not known.

Cougars in both Florida and British Columbia have been found infected with feline immunodeficiency virus (FIV), a virus related to the deadly human HIV. When the B.C. Ministry of the Environment issued blood-collection kits to each cougar hunter in the province, they found that the disease was spread provincewide and was more prevalent in male cats, just as is the case with house cats. FIV reduces the animal's white blood cell count and reduces its ability to fight infections. Any such disease can weaken wild animals, and weak animals in the wild may not survive.

Ken Russell, a Colorado biologist, has pointed out that certain habits of cougars tend to minimize the severity of most diseases. These include the use of dens for only a short period, the lack of bedding in dens, the avoidance of spoiled meat, and the solitary and mobile nature of cougars.

Injuries

It's not unusual for cougars to be injured by their intended prey. In 1970, Maurice Hornocker wrote, "I believe that young lions, particularly when attacking elk, may be injured more frequently than has been believed." Since that time, biologists have recorded a vast array of injuries sustained by hunting cougars. Utah researchers once found a cougar skull pierced by a tree branch, and believe that the unfortunate animal was wounded during a thrashing battle with a deer or elk. Another Utah cougar died of a broken neck; researchers found the decaying bodies of it and its mule deer prey lying together. One young female cougar in southern Alberta died of a broken back sustained during an attack on a mule deer. One male cougar lost his life when he attacked a bighorn sheep, and the momentum of his attack took them both over a ninety-foot cliff. A cougar in Idaho suffered a broken jaw and two broken

canine teeth in a scuffle with a huge bull elk. Most such incidents, of course, are never witnessed.

Occasionally, animals other than prey have been responsible for cougar injuries. In central Idaho, two young cougar kittens were found with crushed skulls, thought to have resulted from the strong talons of golden eagles seen hunting in the area.

At least two cougars in California have died by drowning.

One of the most bizarre injuries on record is that sustained by a young cougar in Utah, which slipped from its perch in a tree, got its head stuck in the fork of the tree, and died in that position.

Cougars seem to go through three main periods of vulnerability to injury or starvation. The first is when the cougars are very young kittens, totally dependent on their mothers and unwise to the numerous dangers in the wild. The second is when the cats are juveniles and have just left their mothers. These animals are still not adept at hunting, and all too often have not yet learned to fear humans. The last period is when the cougars are very old.

COUGAR MORTALITY

Sheep River, Alberta, 1981–1988

Cause	Males		Females		Total	
	ADULT	SUBADULT	ADULT	SUBADULT		
Hunters	3	3	5	2	**13**	*(59%)*
Male cougars	1			2	**3**	*(14%)*
Unknown			3		**3**	*(14%)*
Illegally killed	1				**1**	*(5%)*
Accident				1	**1**	*(5%)*
Disease				1	**1**	*(5%)*

Source: *Management Plan for Cougars in Alberta*, Alberta Fish and Wildlife Division, 1992

By the age of 8 or 9, many wild cougars' teeth are worn almost to the gums, making it difficult for them to feed. By 10, the canines are usually worn down to at least half of their maximum length. Arthritis, cataracts, and other ailments can also make a cougar's last years a real struggle for survival.

LONGEVITY

Although one captive cougar was reputed to have reached the age of 21 and another was reported to be 19½ years old, in the wild very few cougars reach the age of 12. In one study of thirteen cougars in the Diablo Range of California, the average age of death for males was 6 years; for females, 5 years. (Cougars are aged by sectioning their teeth and counting growth rings.)

Biologists disagree as to which gender usually lives longer. With most wild cats, the males have shorter lives due to their aggressive interactions with others of their kind. But with cougars, some biologists believe that the stress of motherhood gives female cougars a shorter life span. In many ways, the cougar is still a cat of mystery.

THE
GHOST
CAT

▼▼▼

COUGAR TERRITORIES
AND REPRODUCTION

▶▶ TERRITORIES

I n the winter of 1993, an old female cougar began hanging
around the southern shore of Quesnel Lake in central British
Columbia. The cat was thin, and was obviously having a
hard time surviving in the cruel white world of a Canadian
winter. But by May, when the final drifts of snow were gone and
green shoots began to peek through the dead grass, the cat was
spotted again. Not only had she survived the winter, but she had

two kittens with her. She had found a mate, and even if she didn't make it through another winter, her genes would live on.

Cougars, like most cats, are solitary animals that only seek the company of their own kind during the mating season. Of all the big cats, only the lion has a complex year-round social system.

A male cougar's territory may cover 25 to 785 square miles, depending on the availability of food and the type of habitat. A female's territory is about half the size of a male's, contracting when she has new kittens to look after and expanding as her young approach adulthood.

Some of the smallest territories ever recorded were in the lush Big Sur area of coastal California. Male cougars there occupied ranges of twenty-five to thirty-five square miles, and females about eighteen to twenty-five square miles. The lack of food in the drylands of southern Utah has led cougars there to use very large ranges: up to 513 square miles for males and up to 426 square miles for females.

Individual cougar territories tend to be quite flexible, altering with seasonal prey migrations or with adverse weather conditions. For example, cougars will readily change home ranges to follow the seasonal movements of deer herds. In Nevada, one cougar used one mountain range in winter, then moved ten miles away to a summer territory in another mountain range. It's also common for cougars to follow deer to lower elevations in the winter. In general, winter ranges are smaller than summer.

The territories of male cougars often overlap those of females in order to provide maximum breeding potential. One enterprising male cougar in southern Alberta stacked the odds in his favor by choosing a territory that overlapped those of eight females. Rarely does a male cougar's territory overlap those of other males.

Males will defend their territories against other comers, but few such encounters occur because cougars mark their territories with signs called scrapes and scratches. There are exceptions, of course: Cougars in both New Mexico and Florida have been found to be very aggressive toward others of their kind. In both areas, it appears that a lack of food and territory has led to numerous cat fights, many of them fatal.

Scrapes are simple depressions dug into the ground and covered with dirt, leaves, and debris. They may be 5 to 15 inches long, 5 to 10 inches wide, and up to 3 inches deep. Biologist Alan Rabinowitz found that in Central America, about half of the cougar scrapes contained cougar urine but no feces. In another study of eighty-six scrapes, only one in five held urine or feces. Cougars sometimes urinate or defecate on top of a scrape, adding an obvious visual sign to what is primarily an olfactory signal. Scratches are made on trees, stumps, or other vertical objects.

A number of other big cats also use such mechanisms, but the exact purpose of them has long been debated. One of the most poetic interpretations was an early myth stating that cougar urine

COUGAR TERRITORIES IN NORTH AMERICA

Area	Male's Territory (average)	Female's Territory (average)	Year of Study
British Columbia	57 sq. mi.	21 sq. mi.	1988
California	58	25	1980
Wyoming	199	42	1983
Arizona	117	42	1973
Nevada	138	49	1979
Alberta	139	60	1988
New Mexico	113	76	1978
Idaho	172	102	1973
Utah	314	260	1984
Texas	392	392	1976

hardened into a precious gem called lincurius and that a cougar covered his urine to hide this gem from humans.

The earliest biologist to investigate cougar markings was Charles Darwin, who observed tree scratches made by jaguars and thought they were likely used to mark the animals' home ranges. Later observations of a number of big cats suggest that Darwin may not have been quite right.

Kailash Sankhala, an Indian biologist, determined that with tigers, "spraying urine…is a spacing mechanism and not a territorial pillar-marking system." In a four-year study of the rare snow leopard, Rodney Jackson also determined that urine-soaked scratches were a mutual-avoidance system. He wrote in *Vanishing*

A COUGAR SHARPEN-
ING ITS CLAWS ON
A LOG
(© LYN HANCOCK)

Tracks that "the cats' elaborate scent-marking system does not serve a territorial purpose; instead, it probably serves to maintain familiarity and distance between individuals, and to attract pairs during the brief mating season." His careful observations did in fact confirm that these markings increased during the breeding season and are most common along the boundaries of male cats' territories. Studies in the Idaho Primitive Area confirmed that male cougars made scrapes more frequently along home range boundaries as well. In British Columbia, one old male cougar who lived on a small island was found to have made no scratches or scrapes; he was the lone resident of the island and there was no reason to advertise his presence.

Some sites seem to be remarkably popular as message-posts. In British Columbia, one conservation officer reported seeing nine scrape piles under one old hemlock tree. Studies in Utah found that most scrape piles were under large trees in saddles, in drainages, or on ridgetops.

An often-overlooked benefit of such spacing messages is that they prevent bloodshed among cougars. Equipped with daggerlike teeth and scimitar claws, two big male cougars could seriously injure each other in a fight. Mutual avoidance is one mechanism for avoiding bloodshed and preserving cougar numbers over the long term.

Although true scrapes seem to be made only by male cougars, there have been reports from Utah of female cougars using mounds of buried scat as some sort of visual sign. Frequently, the mounds are placed under large trees, enhancing their effectiveness as signposts. If unrelated adult female cougars meet, snarls and threats usually suffice to separate the two, although fights do occur. One 4-year-old female in Utah was killed and eaten by another female, who returned repeatedly to the kill site. Such cannibalism is quite rare among females, but it's not uncommon for adult males to eat kittens.

In any given cougar population, the females tend to outnumber the males. The Sheep River cougar study in southern Alberta documented a ratio of about 1 male to 2.5 females; this is similar to ratios found in other cougar studies across the continent. The skewed figure is due partially to the smaller ranges used by females, but also perhaps to the more tolerant nature of the female cat.

❯❯❯DENSITIES

The spacing that results from the use of scrapes and scratches varies widely. One of the highest cougar densities ever recorded was in the Patagonia region of southern Chile, where Iowa State University biologist William Franklin documented densities of 1 cat per 2.7 square miles. In North America, one of the densest populations is in Colorado, where a two-county survey revealed 1 cougar per 8 square miles. At the opposite end of the spectrum, parts of Utah cougar country contain 1 cougar per 77 square miles.

Cougars are quite capable of sustaining established densities after human interruptions. In Idaho, over the winter of 1971 to 1972, twenty-six out of about thirty cougars in a study area were shot by hunters. Over the next six years, another thirty-nine cats were killed. However, biologists were amazed to find that the density of cougars was unchanged because transient cats moved in quickly to fill the empty territories. Transients are independent young cougars, usually between 1½ and 2½ years of age, that have not yet found their own territory or begun to breed.

In most studies of cougar populations, transients make up between 5 and 30 percent of the population. Older transient cats are sometimes found in areas that are not subject to hunting pressures. In the Sheep River cougar study area, for example, where hunting pressure is intense, no transients over 4 years of age were found. Adult resident cats made up 43 to 82 percent of the population; the remainder was composed of juvenile cats and kittens.

When a cougar dies, a transient cat of the same sex is usually quick to take over the vacant territory. Thus, one of the short-term results of cougar culls is to increase the local cougar population as transients move in. As soon as dominant cats stake out their territories, the competing cougars drift away.

Other cat species may also be able to interpret the cougar's scrapes and scratches. When researchers in Vermont sprinkled cougar urine in the woods to attract a cougar reported to be in the area, a local bobcat promptly added his own scrape and feces on top, as if to announce: *Hey, this area's taken, Buster!*

❯ REPRODUCTION

Unlike most mammals, cougars may breed at any time of the year. Most temperate-zone mammals give birth in the spring so that the young are born at the time of maximum food availability. However, in many parts of the western United States, the young cougars are born during June or July. Utah researchers found that most of their cats were born between June and September. Captive cats at the Olympic Game Farm in the state of Washington had peak birth periods in April and August. In Florida, most cougar kittens are born between November and March. In one study in southern Alberta, cougars were born in every month of the year, with almost half born in August and a quarter in winter, between October and March.

Ian Ross, an Alberta cougar researcher, has pointed out that there are a number of advantages to winter births. One is the lack of predators. During the frigid winter months in southern Alberta, bears are in hibernation and pose no threat to defenseless cougar kittens. Winter also results in an abundance of starved and weakened prey for the mother cougar to feed upon, and the deep snow lessens their chance of escape from an attack.

During her 7- to 8-day heat period, a female cougar lets out a bloodcurdling scream that can scare the boots off the most stouthearted hiker, although male cougars seem to find it attractive. In the fall of 1968, Henrik Sepfer and a friend were hunting in the high foothills of southern Alberta. Late one night, both were awakened by an unearthly sound. "I thought some woman was being murdered," says Henrik. "It's hard to believe that an animal can make a sound like that."

Contrary to popular belief, the scream of a female cougar is not meant to startle prey out of cover. Although it's likely that some so-called cougar screams have actually come from other sources—such as great horned owls, which can emit an amazing shriek—the vocalization has been verified in both captive and wild cougars. Researchers in California have even been able to get vocal responses from cougars by playing tape-recorded screams.

A FEMALE COUGAR IN ESTRUS CATERWAULING
(© ERWIN & PEGGY BAUER)

Canadian naturalist R. D. Lawrence once stumbled upon a female cougar in estrus in central British Columbia, and described the cat's wail as "a great banshee scream." John "Grizzly" Adams, who was well used to the awesome roars of his beloved grizzlies, called the cougar's screams "astounding."

When the female and male cougar join up for a duet of passionate bawling, the volume is unbelievable. Anyone who has been unlucky enough to have two amorous house cats under the bedroom window can only imagine the sounds emitted by two 100-pound cougars. R. D. Lawrence described in *The Ghost Walker* a screaming match between two cougars; the female's screams "began in low key as a sort of slow moaning that gradually rose to high pitch." The male, he wrote, "resorted to many growls and snarls, but…the quality of these was different from the more usual angry outcries made by the breed. Intermittently he whistled…the noise volume increased and decreased passionately."

The sound was well known to early pioneers, and was the source of much paranoia. In the late 1800s, a farmer warned the townsfolk of Papinsville, Missouri, about the terrible cougar he had heard screaming downriver. The men locked up their wives, grabbed their guns, and rushed out to kill the advancing menace. Not a shot was fired, however, after the first steamboat to reach the area, the *Flora Jones,* rounded the bend and sounded its piercing whistle.

Female cougars are sexually mature at about 2 to 2½ years and males by about 2½ to 3 years. The difference in ages helps to prevent brother-sister matings, which would weaken the genetic makeup of the wild population.

Maurice Hornocker, the dean of American cougar researchers, believes that "a female will not breed until she is established on a territory." In practice, therefore, breeding females are usually between the ages of 2½ and 9 years. There is, however, one record of a captive cougar giving birth at the age of 12.

The competition for females is intense. Dan Lay, a former predator control officer for Vancouver Island, once watched a small male cougar following a breeding pair. He described the would-be *ménage-à-trois:*

> *This smaller male seemed frustrated. He was making scratches . . . about every 200 yards or so [and] . . . would wander away from the trail of the mating pair then bound back to leave more scratches.*

It's not known if this frustrated feline Romeo was able to attract a mate.

In the wild, it's the female that calls the shots when it comes to breeding. Once a male is attracted, she'll travel with him, hunt with him, and play with him, but if he attempts to mate her before she's ready, she rebuffs him in no uncertain manner. Humans would describe her as coy or flirtatious, but she is, in fact, just obeying her own body's signals, which tell her when the perfect biological moment arrives for mating. Until that time, an overly romantic tom risks a slit ear or slashed nose if he attempts to mount his mate. Normally, a female will only mate with one male during a single breeding cycle. The pair may stay together for several days both prior to and after copulation before drifting apart.

A pair of cougars may copulate up to 70 times per day, an exhausting feat that helps to ensure successful matings during the few days the two are together. Each copulation lasts about a minute. (It's believed by many biologists that the human's more leisurely rate of copulation and the loss of limited heat periods in the human female are the results of the fact that human copulation is not simply used for procreation, but has evolved into a form of social bonding.) When the female cougar's heat period is over, she repels the tom with snarls and with slashes of her razor-sharp claws. After a few boxed ears and swipes across the nose, the amorous male finally gets the message and wanders off.

If she's not impregnated, the female will come into heat again in a month. A female cougar may also have a heat cycle immediately after a litter is lost. It used to be a common practice among certain zoos and game farms to regularly remove cougar litters after about three weeks in order to re-cycle the female. In this way, it was possible to get three litters of kittens each year, which were then sold.

A female cougar will breed successfully on average about every other year. Over her short breeding life, she may only produce four or five young that will survive to adulthood. This is why it's crucial to cougar conservation that hunters remove only males from the population. (Cougars are still hunted legally in all jurisdictions except California and Florida.) Unfortunately, very few jurisdictions in North America prosecute hunters who kill female cougars or even mothers with kittens. In British Columbia, for example, the hunting regulations politely state only that "hunters are requested not to shoot female cougar with kittens."

Despite the fact that hunters prefer the larger male cougars for trophies, one study of hunting statistics in Alberta found that almost half of the cougars shot were females. In Colorado, it has been illegal since 1970 to kill a female cougar with kittens, but wildlife officers there admit that many guilty hunters merely don't report their errors.

Art Good is a hunter and big-game guide in central British Columbia. Prominent among the many stuffed heads and hides on his cabin's walls are the heads of three cougars: one adult female

A RARE PHOTO OF
COUGARS COPULATING
(© ERWIN & PEGGY BAUER)

and two juveniles. "I got those near Tatla [a local lake] in 1958," he says. "Thought I was smart getting three cats at once. But now I haven't seen a cougar for a long time. Guess I wasn't so smart after all."

It's actually quite difficult to distinguish a female from a male cougar in the field, especially if the cat is trapped up a tree. Track size is unreliable, because a young male's tracks can be the same size as an adult female's. Body size is also misleading; adult females and juvenile males are often the same size. The best solution is for hunters to take only animals that are very large, have very large tracks, or whose scrotums are visible when the cat is running or treed. Unfortunately, the current level of knowledge among many hunters leaves a lot to be desired. And as the Alberta government's *Management Plan for Cougars in Alberta* comments, "Shorter seasons and poor snow conditions probably reduce the likelihood of a guide recommending that a treed female be spared."

A horrifying statistic came out of a study of cougars shot by hunters in Utah and Nevada: 41 percent of the adult females shot had kittens when killed. Orphaned kittens under 9 months of age have almost no chance of survival on their own.

A FEMALE COUGAR AND HER TWO YOUNG, KILLED BY HUNTERS IN CENTRAL BRITISH COLUMBIA, 1945–1946 (COURTESY BRUCE HAINES COLLECTION)

The gestation period for cougars lasts for 90 to 96 days. Two or three kittens comprise the average litter, although there is a record of six in a litter from Utah. It's unlikely that such a large litter would ever survive in the wild. If it's the mother's first litter, a single kitten is not unusual.

The birthing den is a simple rock overhang, a shallow cave, or a thicket of vegetation. I once stumbled across a cougar den located high on a rocky slope in the Quesnel Highlands of central British Columbia. The den was framed by two boulders capped with a slab of rock that neatly created a small triangular gap beneath, forming a sort of natural Druid arch. In the dust in front of the den, I found tracks that suggested at least one kitten was inside with its mother. Not wishing to disturb them, I quickly left the area, noting that the den opening faced almost due south, allowing the sun's rays to warm it naturally. I also noted that a small mountain brook trickled its way down the steep slope less than a hundred feet from the den.

Cougar dens are often located near water. On Vancouver Island, many cougar dens are close to beaver dams, providing both food and water. The sites seem to be chosen primarily for protection from predators, rather than from the elements. One American researcher found a den site where the mother slept under cover, but the kittens slept out in the snow. There's usually no bedding in the den, although one mother cougar was found to have pulled out soft belly hairs to line her den. Sometimes the mother cougar will move her den, especially if the site has been disturbed.

KITTENS

Cougar kittens weigh about 1 pound at birth, and enter the world with fluffy, spotted coats. Their ears, legs, and tails are very short, minimizing the surface area exposed to freezing temperatures. The kittens also huddle together to reduce heat loss. In one captive litter of three, the kittens began nursing at 13, 17, and 65 minutes after birth, and were vigorously competing for teats the next day.

Captive cougar kittens have been known to die from wounds accidentally inflicted by their littermates in the competition for Mother's teats, but this has not been observed in the wild.

A YOUNG COUGAR
KITTEN ENTRANCED BY
A BIT OF MOSS
(© LYN HANCOCK)

Like all wild cats, cougar kittens are hardy. One Idaho tracker followed the trail of a female cougar that moved her three 6-week-old kittens during winter and deep-snow conditions. At an age when human babies are totally helpless, the three tough kittens followed their mother, jumping into one of her tracks, up over the snow and down into the next track, then back up again, for three long miles.

The spots on cougar kittens' coats disappear at about 6 to 9 months, although occasionally spots on legs and tails are still visible 3 years later. Teeth begin to erupt at about 10 days. Cornflower blue eyes peek open by about 10 to 14 days and change to a golden hue by about 16 months. Cougar milk has about six times more fat than cows' milk, and the young kittens grow quickly. By 8 weeks, a kitten's weight has increased tenfold. The males put on weight faster than the females.

Most of the kittens' time is devoted to either sleep or play. A recent study of domestic cats found that they spent an average of 16 hours daily in sleep, and it's likely that wild cougar kittens do much the same.

In play, kittens attack a bit of fur or a small stick with vigor, rehearsing the survival skills they'll soon depend upon. Chase and tag are perennial favorites among cougar kittens, and "Let's Attack Mom" is always good for a laugh or two. In fact, like their domestic cousins, adult cougars will play as well, tossing sticks and chas-

ing imaginary objects and each other just for the fun of it. One observer reported seeing her two-year-old son throwing sticks to an adult wild cougar, which was jumping out of the way and purring happily. Anthropologist Elizabeth Marshall Thomas once watched a captive cougar repeatedly catching and releasing a tiny fly, apparently just for amusement.

Only recently has play in mammals received much attention from the scientific community. Its role in developing survival skills is well documented, but it seems to serve a number of other functions as well. Certainly one of these is the simple burning off of excess energy. And it's likely that play between a mother and her kittens cements important social bonds.

The female cougar may introduce her young to wild foods at an early age. One California cougar was observed bringing live grasshoppers to her kittens when they were only 30 days old.

A FEMALE COUGAR
AND HER TWO
YOUNG EXPLORE
THE WILDERNESS.
(© ERWIN & PEGGY BAUER)

By 6 weeks, the kittens begin to regularly eat meat, and after about 3 months they're completely weaned. During this period, the female cougar must leave her young to go hunting. In southern Alberta, it was found that mother cougars sometimes left their young for up to thirty hours to search for food. After her young are weaned, a female will sometimes bring chunks of food back to them. To help them feed, the mother will rip off chunks of meat and place them temptingly in front of them. There are few sights in nature so paradoxical as cougar kittens, the very definition of cuteness, scarfing down great bloody divots of fur and flesh.

As they mature, the kittens begin to follow their mother to kill sites, where they often do more playing than eating. Romping around the kill, and fiercely attacking it with their tiny teeth, the young cougars learn the correct way to open up a kill and what parts to go for first. Six-month-old kittens have even been observed trying to help cache a kill, with their puny paws scraping up little more than dust.

By about 9 to 12 months, the kittens are catching small birds and rodents themselves. This is later than some other wild cats: Lion cubs have been known to bring down much larger prey by the age of 5 months.

The impulse to hunt is innate in cougars, as with all cats. When one young female cougar, which was born in a zoo and had never seen live prey before, was placed in an enclosure in Idaho and filmed for a recent documentary, she knew just what to do when an injured elk calf was put in her pen. The unfortunate calf was killed within minutes. Another captive cougar in Colorado that had never hunted before sprang against the glass to get at a stuffed deer at the Denver Museum of Natural History. The cat had been born on a fur farm and raised by humans, but its recognition of prey was instinctive and immediate.

In 1976, G. Bogue and M. Ferrari reported on the response of a 6-month-old captive cougar kitten to a freshly killed deer: "He sighted the deer, then [let] out a high-pitched loud shriek as he leaped upon the deer's back and attempted to kill it." When the kitten found that its baby teeth were just not up to the job, "he immediately switched around to the front of the throat, biting it convulsively for several minutes."

The fierceness exhibited by cougar kittens is surprising. In 1994, a female cougar and her two tiny spotted kittens were cornered in an old barn near Black Creek in central British Columbia. The owner of the barn was awed by the gutsy kittens: "They looked so cute and cuddly, but my God, they were little spitfires!"

Female cougars are attentive mothers, and guard their young closely. Elizabeth Marshall Thomas once tracked a female cougar with three kittens in the wilds of Idaho. The young female came across an abandoned homestead, and ushered her young inside for concealment during the night. "We…found the print of the young mother's body in snow that had drifted through the open door," wrote Thomas. "She had lain in the doorway keeping watch through the night, as any parent would do."

Female cougars communicate with their young through a vast repertoire of moans, chirps, whistles, and chuckles. Filmmaker Jim Dutcher has reported a "coarse and shrill" mourning cry given when a captive female was separated from her kittens. Naturalist Lyn Hancock, who raised four captive cougar kittens, reported a "shrill and piercing, agonized and piteous" distress call when one young cougar was separated from its littermates. When content, both kittens and mother may purr.

Purring is one of the least understood of all forms of cat communication. Most biologists believe that purrs are created in the cat's voice box. Others believe that they result from turbulence in the bloodstream as blood travels up the windpipe. Richard Jakowski of the Tufts University School of Veterinary Medicine believes that purrs are caused by the cat fluttering its soft palate, the lump of tissue at the back of the throat that prevents food from entering the lungs. He has found that cats' palates are longer than necessary for this purpose alone, and contain a muscle that allows cats to vibrate them at will. Captive cougar kittens have been observed to emit squeaky chirps on their first day of life and to purr on their second.

Kittens leave the security of their mother between the ages of 9 and 24 months. In many cases, it's actually the mother who finally abandons her young when they're ready for the big wild world. In southern Alberta, this separation normally takes place during April, May, or June, the months of maximum food availability. Most juveniles wander away to look for new territories, but some may stay within their maternal home range if there's sufficient food available. (Cheetahs will also share a maternal range if there's enough prey.)

Few kittens survive to adulthood: In one California study, 75 percent of the kittens died within their first two years. Another study found that only one of seven litters had more than one kitten survive to the age of 1 year. The most common cause of death is sport hunting. This tremendous rate of attrition is not unusual among wild cats. In Africa, George Schaller found that two out of three lion cubs studied died before their third birthday.

After leaving their mother, young cougars may roam up to four hundred miles away in search of a vacant home range. Male juveniles tend to migrate farther than females.

If kittens stray into a big male's turf, they will likely pay for their innocence with their lives. The males play no role in the rearing of their young, and are not above killing their own kittens. Between 1981 and 1988, twenty-two cougars were followed in a detailed study in the Sheep River region of southern Alberta. During that period, 14 percent of the cats were killed by other cougars. (It's interesting that, in one study of African lion cubs, the same 14 percent were killed by other lions.) In Idaho, when a juvenile cougar kept captive for filming purposes scaled a 12-foot fence and escaped, it was killed immediately by a patrolling tom. If a mature male captures and kills a young cougar, the juvenile is often eaten.

Such cannibalism, of course, serves to ensure that a dominant male's genes will continue on in his territory. The killing of his own kittens seems contradictory, but it's likely that adult males simply do not recognize their own young.

Once a home range is established by a young cat, its attachment to that area can be extremely intense. One radio-collared cougar that was relocated to a new area took off for home immediately. Four months later, he arrived, after a journey of about three hundred miles.

THE
HUNTING
CAT

▼▼▼

THE COUGAR
AS PREDATOR

Much of the cougar's life is one long search for food, gliding through glades and pouring over rocks with a sinuous grace that has impressed even the most hardened scientific observer. Maurice Hornocker has waxed eloquent about the "grace, beauty, independence, and speed" of wild cougars. Orval Pall, a Canadian cougar biologist, once described cougars as the perfect blend of "beauty, strength, intelligence, and ability." Lyn Hancock has writ-

COUGARS ARE
SURPRISINGLY GOOD
SWIMMERS.
(© ERWIN & PEGGY BAUER)

||||

ten that "a cougar is graceful whatever it does—whether walking, running, leaping, or just lying down."

In one night's search for food, a cougar may cover over twenty-five miles. Biologists in southern Chile's Patagonia region have tracked cougars that covered ten miles of rugged terrain in a few hours. In California, researchers following cougars found that they moved at a steady pace of about a half mile per hour.

Like most cats, the cougar usually dislikes entering water, but if the need for food or new territory is strong, it will swim across lakes and ponds. In the past, cougars regularly swam the half-mile gap between Saltspring Island and Vancouver Island; then the local human population boomed and the cats became scarce. Reports exist of five-mile swims between other coastal islands. Unfortunately, occasional saltwater dips wreaked havoc on early radio collars: At least one collared cat on Vancouver Island was inadvertently harmed by its water-soaked collar in 1973. According to a local resident, "The batteries that had operated the tracking device were green and bulging. The animal's neck was raw and infected. It smelled like rotten meat." Radio collars built today are much more sturdy.

The cougar is an opportunistic hunter, taking whatever game is easiest to catch. In most of North America, the main item on the cougar's menu is ungulates (hoofed animals, including deer, moose, and elk). In one southern Alberta study, three-quarters of the local cougars' diet was made up of these three species. One study in Idaho found that the two prime cougar food items there were mule deer and elk.

The cougar's great agility enables it to kill animals many times its own size, and many a 600-pound bull elk has fallen to the quick and cagey cat. Daniel Boone and his brother even reported seeing a cougar tackling an adult buffalo. Maurice Hornocker has stated

A CAREFUL STALK PRECEDES A QUICK POUNCE ON PREY.
(WILLIAM E. RIDEG)

that "for sheer killing ability, I don't think any cat in the world surpasses the mountain lion."

There's some evidence that male and female cougars may choose different prey, with the big toms tackling larger species. In the Sheep River area of southern Alberta, one study found that 85 percent of the winter prey of male cougars was moose calves, whereas females concentrated on the smaller and lighter deer and elk.

In Belize, biologist Alan Rabinowitz found that where the ranges of cougars and jaguars overlapped, the cougar chose prey species that prevented run-ins with the much stronger jaguar. A similar apportioning of prey has been reported in Nepal between the mighty tiger and the weaker leopard. And in Africa, George Schaller found that two predators, the lion and the hyena, even divided up prey according to age. Lions chose prime, mature wildebeest, while hyenas preferred the very young or very old.

Adult cougars may dine on one deer every ten to sixteen days in the winter, and one every three weeks in the summer. A female cougar with kittens to feed may kill once a week to feed her fast-growing young. These figures fly in the face of the exaggerated numbers ingrained in lore and campfire fables. As Maurice Hornocker says, "The idea that cougars are wholesale killers of big game animals is a myth."

THE DEER IS THE PRIME
FOOD OF COUGARS.
(© ROBERT H. BUSCH)

As recently as the 1940s, it was widely believed that predators were the controlling factor on deer and moose populations. Even conservationist Aldo Leopold used reverse logic in 1947 to claim that because explosions in deer numbers were (then) unknown in the presence of predators, the predators themselves must be controlling the deer population. Then, in 1949, half of the cougars were removed from a study area in Utah and researchers were surprised to find that the deer numbers remained the same. Biologists then began to question the established beliefs about the effects of cougar predation.

It wasn't until the early 1970s that a number of studies showed that in most cases, changes in habitat, overhunting by humans, or food conditions were to blame for decreases in prey numbers. In the pioneer study of cougars in Idaho undertaken by Maurice Hornocker, the conclusion reached was "that lion predation is not controlling ultimate numbers of these prey animals." Detailed studies in Utah in 1967 came to the same conclusion. The most recent studies have had the same results.

Although cougars are usually not the controlling factor on ungulate populations, their predations can still be significant. In New Mexico, from 1979 to 1983, wildlife biologists killed sixty-eight cougars in an attempt to protect their desert bighorn sheep from depredation. However, the scientists were startled to discover that the cougar-killing had no effect, and the depredations continued due to immigrant cats.

➤ COUGAR PREY

Besides deer, moose, elk, and bighorn sheep, rounding out the cat's fare is a long list of almost anything catchable and edible: beavers, porcupines, sheep, goats, rabbits, hares, ground squirrels, mice, and even skunks. The fact that cougars can catch the swift antelope is a tribute to the cat's agility. Birds flying low to the ground may be snatched out of the air, and fish have even been swatted out of streams by hungry cougars.

Like house cats, cougars will also eat grass as an intestinal scour, and captive cougars have been observed grazing for up to five minutes at a time. Grass is especially useful in routing out intestinal worms and other live irritants. Some biologists believe that cats also eat grass to obtain minute quantities of folic acid, an essential vitamin that isn't available in a meat-only diet. Folic acid is essential to the production of hemoglobin in the blood; without it, cats may become anemic.

Food choices are often seasonal: In Idaho, cougars spend much

COUGAR PREY IN NORTH AMERICA

Area	Primary Prey	Secondary Prey	Year of Study
Alberta	deer 39%	moose 23%	1981–1989
British Columbia	deer 57%	rabbits/hares 11%	1971
Oregon	deer 64%	rodents 6%	1985
Utah	deer 88%	elk 4%	1987
Florida	wild hogs 42%	deer 28%	1990

of the summer chasing the abundant ground squirrels, then switch to deer in winter. One study in central British Columbia found that cougars readily switched from deer to snowshoe hares when the latter were at the peak of their ten-year population cycle.

There may also be some selectivity for prey of a certain gender, not because the genders taste different, but because they choose slightly different habitats. In Idaho, for example, adult mule deer bucks are eaten more often than does. This is thought to reflect the bucks' preference for broken terrain and higher elevations, which is also the preferred hunting ground for cougars. In Africa, Serengeti lions similarly select male gazelles over females. There, the reason seems to be that, while females run immediately from danger, males hesitate in order to evaluate the threat. And hesitation spells death.

In South America, a cougar may dine on peccaries, monkeys, guanacos, bats, lizards, and even anteaters. From the limited data available, it appears that South American cougars prey more regularly on small animals than their North American counterparts. In one study in Peru, 75 percent of the cougars' diet was composed of rodents. In Chile, 54 percent of the diet is rabbits and hares.

Cougars rarely eat carrion, but, unfortunately, are not above

snatching a dog or cat from a farmyard porch. One cougar killed in Fresno, California, had the remains of five domestic cats in its stomach.

Cougars drink very little free water, as most of their prey's flesh is 60 to 70 percent water by weight. This was noted as early as 1946 by Stanley Young, who wrote, "When water is scarce the puma apparently is capable of existing for long periods without it."

One of the many myths surrounding the cougar is that the big cats drink from the jugular veins of their prey. In 1760, Thomas Jeffreys, writing in *The Natural and Civil History of the French Dominions in North and South America,* stated that "as soon as this hunter comes up with the elk [moose], he leaps upon him, fixes on his neck, round which he twines his long tail, and then cuts his jugular." Similar statements pervaded hunting tales right up until the 1980s. One possible source for such tales is the fact that cougars will lap blood from cuts on themselves and on others.

R. D. Lawrence once observed a young female cougar licking the blood from the ear of her mate: "Twice he moved his head away from her, but she seemed to relish the taste."

➤ HUNTING AND FEEDING
➤ TECHNIQUES

The cougar usually kills large animals by leaping upon their back or side, followed by either twisting their head to the side to snap the neck or biting through the back of the neck. Death is often due to one of the cougar's large canine teeth forcing vertebrae apart and severing the prey's spinal cord. The kill follows a short stalk and a few mighty leaps. If the prey is not caught within two or three long bounds by the cougar, it usually escapes. Contrary to popular myth, cougars do not hang about in trees, waiting to drop upon prey.

R. D. Lawrence once witnessed a cougar attack on a female caribou in central British Columbia, and described the kill in *The Ghost Walker:*

> *He sailed through the air . . . [covering] thirty-two feet in his first enormous leap . . . hitting the cow on the right shoulder with both forepaws. The blow was devastating. The cow's long neck was snapped violently to the right. . . . The cow had been killed by that first mighty, whiplashing blow.*

Most hunting is done during the evenings or early mornings, but one Idaho study found that cougars there hunted almost as much during the day as at night. In California, one bold cougar strolled in broad daylight through a campground with a dead coyote in its mouth. Most cougars, however, prefer to hole up in a cave or under a rock overhang during daylight and await the cover of night. Observers are often amazed at the tiny orifices through which cougars can squeeze: To get into one cave, a female cougar scrunched herself through a hole only six inches across.

Essayist and novelist Barry Lopez once wrote of the silent "conversation of death" between predator and prey, which he called "a ceremonial exchange, the flesh of the hunted in exchange for respect for its spirit." He coined the phrase during his research into predation by wolves, but one example of this in cougars may have been aired a few years ago on a public television program. The film showed a large male cougar that had just killed a bighorn sheep. The cougar lay down beside the dead sheep, face to face, and tenderly patted the sheep's head, as if thanking it for giving up its life.

Very few studies seem to exist into the cougar's prey efficiency, or percentage of prey that's actually captured. Unlike many cats that chase down their prey, cougars only hunt after a careful stalk and pounce. Smaller game is usually killed by one lethal swipe from a giant paw. Cougars might, therefore, be expected to have a higher prey efficiency than those animals that resort to chases. George Schaller found that in Tanzania, lions were successful in catching the swift gazelle only 26 percent of the time. Cheetahs, which are much faster animals, were successful over half of the time. Maurice Hornocker found that in Idaho, if only the final attack was considered, 82 percent of cougar attacks were successful. The success rate is high because cougars must be able to approach their prey quite closely to begin with before they launch their short attack.

The prey is often dragged to a secluded spot to be devoured. Researchers in Utah and Nevada found that their cats sometimes dragged prey up to a thousand feet away from the kill site, no mean feat when the prey weighs much more than the cat itself.

After a kill, a cougar usually plucks away the fur with its teeth and tongue before ripping the carcass open. Unlike humans, cougars often consume the nutritious internal organs first, and only eat the flesh and muscle tissues later. A cougar in California was once observed squeezing out the contents of its prey's small intestine, then dining on the emptied, spaghetti-like organ.

Nutritionist P. P. Scott found that wild cats cannot convert provitamin beta-carotene into fat-soluble vitamin A. Therefore, they must obtain all of their vitamin A directly from the prey they consume. The richest sources of vitamin A in prey animals are the liver, lungs, and kidneys. In captive feeding experiments, Scott found that a meat diet lacking in liver and other organs is also deficient in calcium, iodine, and retinol. Cats fed such diets developed gross skeletal deformities.

Cougars can consume 20 to 30 pounds of meat at one sitting. If a female cougar has juveniles to feed, an entire deer can disappear as one meal. Large kills are often covered with dirt and grass, and dined upon for two to ten days. One cat in Idaho stayed with an elk carcass during a very cold winter for nineteen days, and another in Canada during December visited its kill for over a month. Road crews in central Idaho have uncovered cougar kills cached under deep snow in the middle of remote roads.

The instinct to cache food is of obvious survival value to any wild predator, and it may develop very early. In a three-year study of another solitary cat, the leopard, Joy Adamson determined that the instinct to store food even developed prior to the cat's learning

A DEER KILLED BY A COUGAR ON VANCOUVER ISLAND— NOTE THAT ONLY THE INTERNAL ORGANS HAVE BEEN EATEN
(JEFF MORGAN)

to kill. Adding a covering of dirt and grass also helps to prevent spoilage, although sometimes instinct overrides practicality. One cougar in Arizona killed a deer on a large granite boulder, and left it covered with only a single twig.

Researchers in Alberta have found that their female cougars tend to stay closer to the kill than the males. The latter often eat for a day or two and then go off to hunt and look for females before returning to eat what's left of the kill.

Very little food is wasted at the kill site: Researchers in both British Columbia and Idaho found that cougars consumed almost three-quarters of the carcasses of big-game prey. Often, all that remains of a kill are a few bones, hoofs, and the skull.

As with most predators, the life of a cougar is one of feast or famine. In one study of cougars killed by federal agents in Utah and Nevada, of 401 cougar stomachs examined, almost a third were totally empty.

➤ Effects of Predation ➤ ➤ by Cougars

Like many predators, the cougar is sometimes beneficial to the game populations it preys upon, weeding out the weak, the sick, the diseased, and the very old. In 1937, Frank C. Hibben examined eleven deer killed by cougars in New Mexico and wrote, "Of the eleven deer, all showed abnormal or subnormal characteristics." In one recent study in Idaho, three-quarters of the elk killed by cougars were less than 1½ years old or over 9½. In the Sheep River cougar study in southern Alberta, it was determined that "most moose calves found in the cougar kill sample were in poor condition." And in south-central British Columbia, "very old animals were taken by cougar in a greater proportion than were represented in the mule deer population." Today, biologists call the upshot of removing weaker prey animals the sanitation effect. An

interesting observation was once recorded by Elizabeth Marshall Thomas, who wrote that her paraplegic daughter "has only to roll her wheelchair through a zoo to get the big cats bounding in their cages." She proposes that "the...motion—slow, uneven, and low to the ground—caused lions to regard her differently from the way they regard able-bodied people." The same ability of cats to recognize weakness was once observed at a travel circus, in which the tigers ignored all of the two-hundred-plus people in the audience, but stared intently at a child with Down's syndrome. In Africa, George Schaller has reported that lions have preyed upon humans when the latter were drunk, their unsteady gait showing weakness to the watchful predators.

Predators serve a useful function in preventing prey population explosions—increases that in the long run could strip the carrying capacity of the area and result in massive overgrazing. On Vancouver Island, when the local cougars and wolves were killed off, it was found that the deer tended to gather in small areas and severe overgrazing resulted.

The Zuni were one of the first of Native peoples to recognize the advantageous nature of the cougar's predation: They called the cougar the Father of Game. The European settlers in North America were slower to catch on. As recently as 1913, biologist William T. Hornaday, the director of the New York Zoological Society, stated that "At this moment pumas are a curse to the deer, elk, and other game." This attitude did not change until the 1960s.

Another effect that cougars can have on prey populations is to keep these populations from recovering from the devastations of a bad winter, outbreak of disease, or other crisis. If the prey population is naturally depressed, cougar predation may keep it that way.

➤ INTERACTIONS WITH ➤ OTHER SPECIES

After a kill by cougars, smaller predators such as weasels and ravens hover nearby to scrounge a quick morsel or two. In Yellowstone National Park, packs of coyotes have even been observed to steal prey from cougars.

The cougar's relationship with larger predators is not always so cozy, especially if a skirmish over food occurs.

Bobcats and lynx that try to steal food from their larger cousin do so at their own peril, for both are easily killed by the much more powerful cougar. Tussles with bears are more evenly matched, often with no clear winner. Both combatants usually end up bloodied and bitten, having wasted more calories than the food they were fighting over would have provided. Outdoorsman Ben East, in his book *Bears,* wrote of one confrontation in which a grizzly walked in on a feeding cougar, "which reacted angrily, snarling and spitting. But in the end it fled without giving battle and the grizzly took over the kill."

Cougars also have tremendous respect for wolves. At the turn of the century, a hunter named Felix Michaud wrote that wolves will chase a cougar up a tree:

> *Its fate, in bitter cold weather, will still be very uncertain; for the wolves . . . will watch, in a restless state of action which keeps their own legs limber, until the cougar's feet are frozen, and the animal powerless to cling falls into their waiting jaws.*

Needless to say, this fanciful tale has not been verified by modern biologists, but wolf kills of cougars have been verified recently in the United States. In 1990, a pack of wolves killed a cougar outside Glacier National Park in Montana; there were two similar kills in 1993. The solitary cougar has little chance against a well-drilled pack of wolves, but lone wolves have been killed by cougars in both Alberta and Montana.

➤ THE FEEDING OF COUGARS ➤ IN CAPTIVITY

In captivity, adult cougars eat about 9 pounds of food per day. In the past, rickets was common among captive cougars due to a lack of calcium in the diet. Zookeepers still seem reluctant to feed whole carcasses to their cats, partly for public relations reasons.

To relieve the boredom of captive cats, some zoos have begun to provide simulated hunts for their cats' enjoyment. One of the first to do so was Chicago's Brookfield Zoo. Enlightened keepers there installed a branch that, when climbed upon by the cougars, triggered an electronic signal that sent a plastic marmot scurrying out of a hole and into cover eight feet away. When the cougars rooted about in the marmot's hole, their movements triggered a lever that released a feed of raw meat. The cougars had only 1½ seconds to get to the marmot's hole; if they were too slow, they received no food, just as in wild hunts. It can only be hoped that more zoos will pay more attention to their charges' mental needs and provide similar stimulation for their animals.

WILD CAT, TAME WORLD

▼▼▼

THE COUGAR AND HUMANITY

➤ EARLY ATTITUDES
➤ TOWARD COUGARS

Marking out a small party of hunters or travellers, [the cougar] will follow them for days, and watch their camp at night, till at last it discovers one of their number resting a little separate from his companions. Then, when all is dark and silent, the insidious [cougar] glides in, and the sleeper knows but a short awakening when its fangs are buried in his throat.

These were the words of Lord Southesk, a British traveler to the Canadian west, who recorded his fanciful thoughts in his 1875 journal. But they could have been written by almost any other settler or farmer in

73

the early history of North America. In the good animal/bad animal slots in which nineteenth-century humans placed animals, cougars were thought to be very, very bad.

The first inhabitants of the continent, however, held more reverent views of the big cat. In the Mujica Gallo Gold Museum in Lima, Peru, is a very special artifact. The relic is fourteen inches long and is in the shape of a flattened cougar hide. It was used by the ancient Mochica culture as a vessel to hold coca leaves. It's made of solid gold.

Another South American people, the Tiahuanacans, who flourished in Peru from 200 A.D. to 1000 A.D., respected the cougar as companion of a god. Images abound of a god with vacant eyes and tears flowing down his cheeks, accompanied by a condor and a cougar. This god may have been the creator god Viracocha, placing the cougar in noble company indeed.

A NINETEENTH-CENTURY ENGRAVING OF THE COUGAR, "A VICIOUS AND CUNNING BEASTE"

Two hundred years after the demise of the Tiahuanacans, the heart of Cuzco, the capital city of the Incas, was laid out with reverence in the outline of a crouching cougar. The city sits on a promontory of high ground between two small streams. The junction of the streams was the cougar's tail, the central square of the city was the animal's heart, and its head was the hill above the city. Three huge walls of masonry zigzagged along the hill, forming the teeth of the cougar. Numerous other cougar images survive in Inca relics today. North of Cuzco, near a pass above the Apurimac River, a boulder some fourteen feet across sits guarding the pass. Carved into the surface of the boulder are numerous Inca figures. Prominent among them is the figure of a crouching cougar.

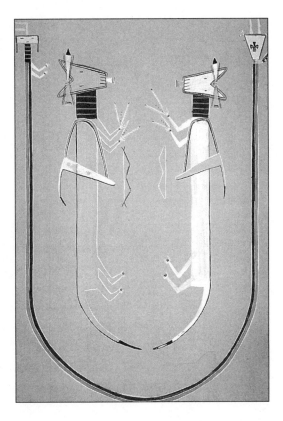

In North America, the Aztecs believed that if you scratched your chest with a bone from an albino cougar, death could be prevented. Other Natives hung a cougar paw over a sick person's head to drive out the evil spirits causing the illness. Cougar galls were similarly consumed in order to exorcise spirits.

The Native peoples of what is now called Baja California watched for buzzards spiraling above cougar kills in order to scrounge a meal. The Cheyenne had a legend in which a cougar kitten was suckled by a human female, then in maturity became a provider of food to its foster tribe. The Navajo believed that the cougar helped to feed them, purposely leaving portions of its kills for them to eat. As recently as the early 1900s, western writer Zane Grey wrote of a Navajo guide refusing to participate in a cougar hunt in the belief that the cougar was a Navajo deity.

A 1929 NAVAJO SAND PAINTING OF TWO MOUNTAIN LIONS (WHEELWRIGHT MUSEUM OF THE AMERICAN INDIAN, P19·#3)

The Apaches believed that cougar screams denoted the death of a tribal member.

Many Plains Natives used animals to represent the four cardinal points of the compass: The bear stood for the west, the bobcat the south, the wolf the east, and the cougar the north.

The Miwok of California described the cougar as the ideal hunter: strong, independent, and brave. The Cougar Society of Zia Pueblo in New Mexico believed that cougar spirits helped them in the hunt. Natives of Cochiti Pueblo could only become members of the Opi warrior society by killing the greatest of hunters—the cougar. Zuni tribe members carried a stone cougar fetish with them to ensure hunting success.

▸Bounties and Management of Cougars

When the Europeans arrived in the New World, they brought with them the attitudes of a people used to exterminating animals as potential competitors for land and game. Jesuit priests in California in the 1500s offered Natives a bull for each cougar killed. In 1609, Henry Spelman of the Jamestown colony in Virginia wrote that "ther be in this cuntry Lions, Bears, [and] woulves," but that soon changed.

The first bounty on cougars was established in 1680, and was quickly followed by many others. In 1694, Connecticut offered a bounty of twenty shillings for each dead "catamount." South Carolina's Act for Destroying Beasts of Prey, enacted in 1695, forced Native American hunters to submit a predator's hide annually or be whipped in punishment. Massachusetts enacted a bounty payment of forty shillings per cougar in 1742.

All too often, these bounties were used as justification for the wholesale slaughter of predators. One American bounty hunter, Ben Lilly, boasted that he had killed over a thousand cougars in his career and bragged that he would have done so even without being paid for it. Many of the early bounties on cougars were not eliminated until the arrival of the environment-friendly 1960s. In

Canada, Alberta had cougar bounties until 1964. The last state to have a cougar bounty was Arizona, which did not remove it until 1970.

Little was known about wildlife management prior to the 1960s, and the result of large-scale removal of predators was often catastrophic. In the early 1900s, for example, Arizona officials decided to kill off the cougars, coyotes, and bobcats from the Kaibab Plateau in order to "improve the hunting for humans." The result was disaster. Without the limiting effect of natural predation, the deer population exploded from three thousand in 1910 to over a hundred thousand by 1924, and the area was soon overgrazed. Deer died by the thousands, and many of the overgrazed lands never grew back. The cougar did not return for almost fifty years.

Although desert oracle Edward Abbey once wrote, "The mountain lion eats sheep. Any animal that eats sheep can't be all bad," his view was not shared by most of the early ranchers, who demanded that the federal government remove cougars from their grazing ranges on demand. Their feelings were exemplified by an 1885 article in *Forest & Stream* magazine, which bluntly stated that "the panther should be systematically pursued and destroyed." Sadly, this is just what the federal animal control agents did.

A MINERAL COUNTY, MONTANA, BOUNTY HUNTER, BEN VOGLER, 1927
(MONTANA HISTORICAL SOCIETY)

Between 1937 and 1977, U.S. federal authorities officially killed over ten thousand cougars, although some claim that the actual toll was much higher. Earlier records are even fuzzier. (The Animal Damage Control program actually began in 1915. It was given sweeping powers for "the destruction of mountain lions, wolves, coyotes,...and other animals injurious to agriculture, horticulture, forestry, husbandry, game, or domestic animals, or that carried disease.") One naturalist tallied up bounty records and found that, in addition to the federal kills, over two hundred thousand cougars were killed by bounty hunters between 1900 and 1970.

The situation in Arizona in the early days was typical. The state had for years considered the cougar to be vermin, an animal to be destroyed at every opportunity. Between 1918 and 1947, over two thousand cougars were killed. In 1947, the state began to offer a bounty that ranged up to $100 per cat, a huge sum for the day. The result was that between 1947 and 1969, over five thousand cougars were killed. The bounty was dropped the next year.

In an address at Yale in 1913, William T. Hornaday, the director of the New York Zoological Society, told students that "the eradication of the puma from certain districts that it now infests to a deplorable extent is a task of immediate urgency." With even the biological community against it, the cougar didn't stand much of a chance.

It's easy to dismiss the early carnage as a by-product of the antiquated Victorian attitudes toward wildlife. But few people are aware that the widespread killing of predators is a modern phenomenon as well. The continued existence of the war waged on predators was little known until 1990, when a disgruntled U.S. Fish and Wildlife Service employee published a photo of the heads of thirteen cougars killed by federal agents in Arizona. The U.S. Department of Agriculture's Animal Damage Control Department (now known euphemistically as Wildlife Services) still kills over two hundred cougars each year, part of their annual toll of over two *million* "nuisance" animals.

THE HEADS OF ELEVEN COUGARS KILLED BY FEDERAL OFFICIALS FOR PREDATION IN ARIZONA
(COURTESY WILDLIFE DAMAGE REVIEW)

))))

The Animal Damage Control Department's gung-ho attitude toward the killing of predators has come under fire recently as ex-agents have come forth with shocking inside stories on the organization. The killing of predators costs taxpayers $30 million per year, and the cost-effectiveness of many of the ADC's activities is questionable. In one well-publicized case, ADC trappers spent over three weeks killing fifty-six animals, including innocent deer, skunks, badgers, porcupines, and foxes, after a rancher complained of a coyote killing *one* of his lambs.

In another instance, an ADC agent was found guilty of illegally killing eagles in Texas. The man was fired and sentenced, but a few years later was quietly rehired by the Wyoming office of Animal Damage Control.

The Humane Society of the United States, the Sierra Club, and Defenders of Wildlife have all spoken loudly and angrily about the misadventures of the Animal Damage Control Department. Ex-agent Dick Randall has published horrifying photos of animals tortured with gas, wire hooks, poison, and leg-hold traps. He has condemned what he calls "decades of useless slaughter," and his pleas are echoed by Tucson-based Wildlife Damage Review (WDR).

Review personnel are especially critical of the fact that many of the killings are on public lands, lands theoretically owned and controlled by taxpayers. "Why do ranchers who graze their cattle on public land enjoy the benefits of a welfare system that not only leases them land at ridiculously low rates, but also protects their inventory from wildlife attacks?" asks WDR's Marion Baker-Gier-

Cougars Killed by Animal Damage Control, 1994			
California	71	Arizona	14
Utah	70	Colorado	8
Nevada	54	New Mexico	8
Texas	46	Idaho	4
Oregon	15	Montana	3
Total			**293**

lach. "Maybe the lion can never really lie down with the lamb, but the two at least ought to be able to coexist."

➤ LIVESTOCK PREDATION
➤ BY COUGARS

Although Theodore Roosevelt once described the cougar as "a big horse-killing cat," livestock predation by cougars in most parts of North America is actually quite rare. Canada's prime cow country is in southern Alberta, where an average of only five predations by cougars per year has occurred over the past decade, despite the hundreds of thousands of cattle raised in the province. Offending cougars are usually relocated, unless they're unusually aggressive or in poor physical condition; in these cases they are either shot or humanely euthanized.

In most of the United States, predation by cougars is equally uncommon. In Idaho, even though cougar habitat is now grazed by both cattle and sheep, Maurice Hornocker has noted that reports of livestock predation by cougars are rare to nonexistent. In Nevada, one researcher has even reported that cougars were tracked right through a number of sheep pastures without one case of predation.

The worst stock predation seems to be in the southwestern United States, where young calves are the main target. Offending animals in the U.S. are usually shot. In Arizona, for example, thirty-eight cougars were killed as stock-killers in 1993. Although individual ranchers can suffer heavy losses from predation by cougars, even in the Southwest overall losses are low. In New Mexico, for example, verified predations by cougars affect less than 1 percent of ranchers each year.

Improved livestock husbandry practices, such as keeping calves in enclosed pastures and the use of guard dogs, could go a long way toward reducing predation by cougars, but open grazing, often on cheaply leased federal lands, is a well-established norm in the southern states. American cougar researcher Fred Lindzey has advised that "pasturing livestock, primarily sheep, in more open areas, and avoiding timbered areas, particularly those in steep, broken terrain should reduce livestock losses to cougars."

Currently, both Colorado and Wyoming pay financial compensation for cougar predation on livestock. In each state, the total annual compensation is less than $50,000 per year. Both states class the cougar as a game animal and encourage its hunting. In fact, compensation isn't paid in either state if the landowner doesn't allow hunting on his property.

In most parts of North America, the cougar has now been upgraded from the varmint list to the big-game list, which provides more control over its conservation. Of all the political jurisdictions in North America with resident cougars, only Texas still has an open cougar season—due primarily to the powerful ranching interests in that state. All that's required in Texas is a valid hunting license and, if the cougar is shot on private property, the landowner's permission.

In 1991, the Lone Star Chapter of the Sierra Club filed a petition with the Texas Parks and Wildlife Department asking for the re-classification of the cougar as a protected nongame species. The petition set out exceptions for cats attacking humans, but the department stuck to its guns—literally. In 1994, records show that 158 cougars were officially shot in Texas, but since the reporting is done only on a voluntary basis, it's estimated that the actual toll was closer to 200.

Ranchers in neighboring New Mexico have long tried to get the cougar removed from their state's big-game list and put back on the varmint list. In 1983, legislators tried to push House Bill 365 through the legislature to do just that. After a stormy session, the bill was tabled in committee.

Ray Stiles, a park naturalist with Big Bend National Park, says that ranchers see the cougar as "a competitor to be eradicated in the best interests of their business, to protect their livestock. I do admit, though, that many consider it a macho thing to kill a cougar."

►Cougar Attacks
►on Humans

Cougar predation on humans is even more rare, and is contrary to the cat's nature. In 1892, Francis Parkman wrote that "the mountain lion shrinks from the face of man"; even Theodore Roosevelt admitted in 1901 that instances of the cat having attacked humans "are exceedingly rare." Biologist Alan Rabinowitz, who has studied wild cats from Belize to Bhutan, describes the cougar as "a very unaggressive cat."

But there have been exceptions, and reports of cougar attacks on humans, in areas with large populations of both humans and cougars, have increased. In the past century, cougar attacks in North America have resulted in the deaths of eleven people. Three of these deaths occurred within a two-year period from 1994–1995.

In 1986, five-year-old Laura Small was searching for tadpoles in a creek in Caspers Wilderness Park in southern California when she was suddenly grabbed by a cougar and dragged off. A hiker beat off the animal with a stick and the terrified girl was rushed to the hospital. As a result of her encounter, Laura lost the sight in one eye and is partially paralyzed. Her family sued the county authorities and was awarded preliminary damages of $2 million, the jury ruling that the county had not adequately warned tourists of the potential danger of cougars in the park.

The award sent shock waves through the wildlife management community across North America, which scrambled to erect signs and issue booklets to wilderness hikers. Today, visitors to Caspers Wilderness Park must sign a liability waiver prior to hiking through the park, and minors are not allowed in certain park areas. Similarly, hikers in Montana's Glacier National Park are now often faced with foreboding signs stating: CAUTION: MOUNTAIN LION ON TRAIL. Park managers aren't taking any chances.

It has long been known that cougars will feed upon human flesh. Bernal Diaz del Castillo, who accompanied Cortéz to Mexico in 1519, reported that the cougars in Montezuma's zoo were fed "deer, chickens, little dogs,...and also on the bodies of the Indians they sacrifice." The first recorded lethal cougar attack on a white man in North America appears to have been upon one Philip Tanner in Pennsylvania in 1751.

Despite folklore to the contrary, rabies is almost unknown among cougars. Only one cougar attack in North America, a California case in 1923, may have been attributable to rabies. Of the over eight thousand cases of rabies in North America reported to the Centers for Disease Control and Prevention in Atlanta, Georgia, in 1995, there was not one instance of rabies in cougars.

Almost a third of all cougar attacks in North America have occurred on Vancouver Island. Dan Lay, the former predator control officer for Vancouver Island, described the island's cats as "by far the most vicious cougars in all of [British Columbia]....Over 50 percent of the cougars I take from settled areas have been scarred up by fighting." Lay suggests that adult male cougars may be pushing juveniles out of occupied territories and into conflicts with humans.

However, Knut Atkinson, a carnivore biologist with the British Columbia Wildlife Branch, doesn't believe that the Vancouver Island cougars are more aggressive than any others. He explains the situation this way:

> Many of our attacks, and all of the fatalities, have taken place on the west coast of the Island. This is the area where our deer populations are the lowest, due to a combination of poorer habitat, logging, and wolf predation, and where people and their houses are right against the bush. There is no buffer zone.... Occasionally a child is in the wrong place at the wrong time and we have an attack.

Some of the early recorded "attacks" on Vancouver Island, however, are open to question. In 1934, a Vancouver Island hunter killed a cougar and was shocked to find scraps of blue cloth and brass buttons in the cat's stomach. He immediately assumed that a sailor had been eaten by a cougar and hunters began roaming the woods searching for more of the man-eaters. Three cougars were killed before a local resident came forth and sheepishly admitted that the scraps of cloth belonged to a whale-oil soaked jacket that he'd thrown away, and that had been scrounged from the garbage by an enterprising cougar. Despite his admission, old-timers still talk of the "man-eating cougars" that ravaged their community in the 1930s.

Of those attacks verified by biologists, many are made either by old, starving animals or by young cougars still learning to hunt. In one British Columbia study, most attacks were by juvenile cougars independent of their mothers but not yet proficient at catching prey.

A COUGAR DRINKING FROM THE OCEAN ON THE BRITISH COLUMBIA COAST
(© LYN HANCOCK)

Almost half of the cats known to have attacked humans were underweight juveniles, animals that were desperate for food. Half of the offending adult cats were also noticeably thin.

Other attacks have been made by female cougars attempting to protect their young. Ian Ross, a cougar researcher in southern Alberta, once came across a female cougar that uttered a low moan and began to walk slowly toward him. "Then she broke into two or three very fast steps toward me and I thought, 'This is it!' I just shrieked at her and waved my arms, and she stopped,…turned, and then very slowly walked out of my way," he says. He later found that she had two newborn kittens, and had just been trying to defend them. "I don't fault her at all," he adds.

By far the majority of attacks by cougars are on children, whose small size is not dissimilar to that of the cougar's natural prey. Cougar researcher Fred Lindzey has theorized that a child's "quicker, more erratic movements compared with adults" also make them vulnerable. Children between five and nine years of age seem to be at highest risk.

Kailash Sankhala, an Indian tiger biologist, found that "tigers

A JUVENILE COUGAR
ON VANCOUVER
ISLAND—NOTE THE
SCRATCHES ON ITS
NOSE FROM SCRAPS
WITH OTHER COUGARS
(© KNUT ATKINSON)

start stalking as soon as they find a man in a bent position, but when he stands up they lose interest." R. L. Eton reached a similar conclusion in his studies of the cheetah.

The cougar, too, seems to find an adult human in a standing position just too tall to be considered fair game. Of the few adults who have been attacked, many have been crouching at the time. One hunter met a cougar a few years ago on a logging road near Vancouver, British Columbia. The two held a staring contest for a few minutes, but the cat made no move until the hunter bent over to pick up a rock. Only when he was in this crouched position did it attack. He was able to beat the cougar off with his hands; he wasn't even scratched.

In 1993, a female jogger near Sacramento was attacked and killed by a cougar, following a similar attack in Colorado three years earlier. The cat was tracked down and killed; she was found to be a lactating mother, with a 1-month-old cub hidden nearby. The reason the woman was killed, though, is likely because she was running.

Running triggers a chase instinct in almost all predators, even in cougars, which normally avoid standing, two-legged prey. The same instinct goes awry when the prey is confined and continues running in panic. There's a report from Arizona of a cougar entering a sheep pen and killing all twenty sheep in one night. One Alberta cougar similarly killed fourteen goats during a single evening. Although these are often cited as examples of the cougar's "bloodthirsty" nature, they're actually just examples of the cat obeying a predatory chase instinct under unusual conditions. Cougars simply don't understand that domestic animals are not fair game.

Dr. Paul Beier, Associate Professor, Wildlife Ecology Department, Northern Arizona University, made a study of cougar attacks on humans and presented his findings to the cougar conference sponsored by the Colorado Division of Wildlife in Denver in 1991. He found that most of the attacks came from behind, followed by a bite to the back of the neck. Most of the people who were attacked weren't aware of being stalked until the stab of pain. Dennis Pemble, a wildlife conservation officer in southern British Columbia, believes that "a cougar is most likely to attack when it believes its prey is not aware of its presence...or if the prey does not indicate it will fight back, such as someone running away."

Two things are notable about these attacks on humans: their rarity, and the reaction of many humans to the mere presence of cougars or other predators. After one cougar attack near Colorado Springs, a number of residents demanded that all cougars within 150 miles of town be shot. Following a recent grizzly attack in Alberta, an indignant citizen wrote to the local paper demanding that all the bears in the *entire province* be shot. "Why should the public have to put up with this when we only want to enjoy the countryside?" another complainant wrote. Luckily, most wilderness hikers take a more tolerant view of the wild predators they might meet on the trail.

It's interesting, though, that the mysterious nature of the cougar has in some cases led to an animosity that's not directed toward other, better-known predators. In 1991, a cougar attacked a dog in a kennel near Colorado Springs, but quickly left the scene when a neighbor fired shots at it. According to Robert B. Davies, of the Colorado Division of Wildlife, the first reaction of the dog's owners was "to request removal of all mountain lions." It was patiently explained to them that this was not possible. Davies noted that "these people had had black bears feeding out of the garbage cans the previous summer and were not concerned about bears."

In one Colorado study of cougar attacks, researchers found that of seventy-one interactions with pets, cougars attacked in 61 percent of the cases. In the interactions between cougars and humans without pets, the chance of a person being attacked was found to be about 1 in 2.2 million.

One of the most controversial problems today is that of the cougar population in California. In 1994, seven cougars in California were killed as nuisance animals; two of them had attacked humans. It's estimated that the state now contains about five thousand cougars, twice that of only twenty years ago.

Cougars in California were classed as varmints until 1963, under a very generous bounty program. Hunters received $50 to $60 per cat, plus expenses, which averaged an additional $500 to $600. The program was discontinued in 1963, when cougars were classed as nongame animals. In 1969, they were reclassed as game animals for a two-year period. After over a hundred cats were shot, the species was given protection until 1987. A sport-hunting season was then opened on cougars for a short period, until it was challenged under the California Environmental Quality Act. In 1990, California citizens passed Proposition 117, the California Wildlife Protection Act, which banned cougar hunting completely. The only cats that can now be legally shot under depredation permits are nuisance animals—those that have caused damage to humans, livestock, or property.

Theoretically, the damage caused by a cougar in California must be reported and verified by Department of Fish and Game personnel before a depredation permit is issued. However, almost two hundred such permits have been issued annually since 1990, many of which are based on mere cougar sightings. For example:

♦May 1994. A hiker in Cuyamaca Rancho State Park is followed by a curious cougar. Authorities deem it a threat and shoot it.

♦August 1994. A cougar strolls into a parking lot in Montclair and hides under a car. It, too, is deemed "dangerous" and is shot by wildlife officers.

♦August 1994. A young female cougar wanders into a backyard in Loomis. Local police surround the frightened animal and shoot it, stating that it's acting "aggressively."

Almost half of the depredation permits issued in California since 1990 have resulted in the destruction of a cougar.

Some of the killings of cougars, of course, were justified. There have been two recent deaths resulting from cougar attacks in California. A jogger was killed in a state park near Sacramento in 1993, and a hiker in Cuyamaca Rancho State Park was killed in late 1994. Since 1990, California has reported eight cougar attacks on humans, including these two deaths.

The problem is there is not room for five thousand cougars in California. With a human population of over thirty million, and rural development creeping up every available canyon, conflicts with wildlife are bound to occur. Some biologists also believe that the cougars are losing their fear of humans. "We're seeing a different kind of mountain lion," says Paul Wertz, information officer with the California Department of Fish and Game. "They used to stay in remote areas and had enough contact with hunters and dogs that they learned to avoid them. But today they are no longer threatened by those sources."

There is also a concern about the effect of cougar predation on the threatened California bighorn sheep, which was reintroduced to the state in 1971, at the exorbitant cost of over $2,200 per animal. Biologists are perhaps justifiably concerned about protecting their investment.

Inevitably, some people have called for the retraction of Proposition 117. Although amending this proposition requires a four-fifths vote in both houses of the legislature, it can be altered by the enactment of additional propositions. An attempt to retract the proposition in March 1996 failed by a narrow margin, despite a strong pro-hunting lobby.

Steve Torres, a biologist with the California Department of Fish and Game, has stated that "there is no biological reason not to hunt mountain lions. Lions in California are not endangered or threatened and are not in jeopardy." But supporters of the original Proposition 117 point out that California's high ratio of humans to cougars is the real problem; sparsely populated states like Oregon, which has over twenty-five hundred cougars, have never experienced a single mauling or fatality caused by cougars. The advocates would therefore prefer to see aggressive cats moved to remote parks to reduce human-cougar conflicts. They also point out that there's a small population of cougars living within the Santa Monica Mountains in Los Angeles County, within an hour's drive of one of the largest cities in the world, and that not one of these cats has ever harmed a human. Biologists theorize that these cats have learned that humans are dangerous and should be avoided.

Some wildlife officers in other states, however, believe that the opposite is happening—that their cougars are starting to lose some of their natural fear of humans due to the high numbers of hikers and people who live in rural areas. Keith Aune, of the Montana Department of Fish, Wildlife, and Parks, found that "habituated mountain lions…begin to feed on livestock, human refuse…and, in some cases, pets in residential areas. Several…completely lost fear of humans."

Many so-called cougar attacks are nothing more than examples of the cat's innate curiosity. Alberta cougar biologist Martin Jalkotzy documented one case in which a cougar chased a girl up a tree then ran up, touched her with its nose, and ran off, its curiosity satisfied. Recently, a young cougar strolled onto private land near the town of Priddis in southern Alberta only to be quickly repelled by a farmwife wielding a broom. In the ensuing scuffle, the woman was bitten. The headlines in the local paper the next day screamed: COUGAR ATTACKS WOMAN! Jalkotzy commented that this is the usual slant that the media takes. "It would be more accurate," he noted, "for the headline to have read WOMAN ATTACKS COUGAR!"

Another recent incident involved a man in southern British Columbia who fell asleep in the woods and awoke to find himself under scrutiny by a cougar only four yards away. The two watched each other surreptitiously for a few minutes, but when the man made direct eye contact, the cougar quietly walked away.

Eye contact seems to repel many members of the cat family. In India, residents of the Sundarban marshes were regularly preyed upon by tigers until researchers discovered a simple deterrent. It seemed that tigers wouldn't attack a person wearing a mask on the back of his or her head, and the foresters and honey collectors lived for a while without fear. But cats are intelligent, and as soon as they discovered that the staring faces were not real, the attacks resumed.

In *Wild Hunters: Predators in Peril,* American cougar researcher Jay Tischendorf has stated:

> *Humans have a way of getting themselves into bad situations*
> *with any kind of wildlife from rattlesnakes to chipmunks and*

squirrels. I think probably every animal in the world at one point or another has "attacked humans," but probably it almost always relates to the person being in the wrong place at the wrong time.

And the hordes of hikers now inundating America's last wilderness areas ensure that such inadvertent encounters will continue.

So just what *do* you do if you come face to fang with a cougar? One British Columbia pioneer recommended, "Never run....Bang two rocks together as loud as you can." Maurice Hornocker has similar advice: "Stand firm, fight back, and yell." Ken Russell, leader of the Colorado Cooperative Wildlife Research Unit, adds that "giving the lion sufficient time and room to escape is important."

However, the chance of such an encounter is very slim. Statistically, you're five hundred times more likely to be stung by a bee and almost a thousand times more likely to be zapped by lightning than you are to be attacked by a mountain lion.

➤ Cougar Hunting

Cougars have been hunted by humans since before the arrival of Europeans in the New World. The Incas used to hunt the cats using soldiers, who encircled the animals and drove them into a central area, where they were speared and stoned. In Argentina, bolas were used to rid ranches of cougars. Until the 1960s, many South American ranchers employed *leoneros,* or "lion hunters," to shoot any cougars that strayed onto private ranches. In North America, cougars have been speared, trapped in pits, poisoned, and shot. The advent of snowmobiles and off-road vehicles in the 1960s meant increased access to once-wild areas and increased sport hunting of cougars.

Cougars were not hunted for sport to any great degree until after World War II, when it became popular to pursue the animal with hounds and shoot it once treed. Many hunters considered the cougar the ultimate prize, a prime badge of hunting ability. During the 1950s alone, one outfitter in the American Southwest, Robert McCurdy, claimed to have shot over a thousand cougars, describing his conquests in a book modestly entitled *Life of the Greatest Guide*. As late as 1965, one hunting magazine editor described a cougar hunt as "the most spectacular and exciting hunt of all." In 1992, the Fish and Wildlife Division of the Alberta government called the hunting of cougars a "quality recreational experience."

Today, society's values have matured, and many people question how much sport is involved in shooting a placid cougar out of a tree.

Cougars are currently hunted in British Columbia, Alberta, Montana, Idaho, Washington, Oregon, Colorado, Wyoming, Arizona, New Mexico, and Texas. Over three thousand cougars a year are shot by hunters, with the largest hunting harvest in Montana. The current Boone and Crockett Club–record cougar is one shot in 1979 near Tatlayoko Lake in central British Columbia.

BOONE AND CROCKETT CLUB TROPHY COUGARS
(TOP FIVE TROPHY COUGARS)

Score	=	Greatest Length of Skull	+	Greatest Width of Skull	Location	Year
16$4/16$"		9$9/16$"		6$11/16$"	Tatlayoko L., B.C.	1979
16$3/16$"		9$8/16$"		6$11/16$"	Idaho Co., ID	1988
16"		9$4/16$"		6$12/16$"	Garfield Co., UT	1964
15$15/16$"		9$1/16$"		6$14/16$"	Clearwater R., Alta.	1973
15$14/16$"		9$2/16$"		6$12/16$"	Walla Walla Co., WA	1988

(courtesy Boone and Crockett Club)

In most parts of the cougar's range, there exist no accurate estimates of cougar numbers; government hunting quotas are set according to fuzzy, out-of-date figures. And there's an urgent need for legal protection of female cougars or mothers with kittens in all areas. Despite the many natural hazards of life in the wild, sport hunters in North America kill more cougars than anything else.

Today, many hunters are switching to grabbing a quick photo or two instead of killing their prey. Typical of the new breed of cougar guide is John Langton of Vernon, British Columbia. For six years now his guiding service has taken hunters into the rugged Shuswap River drainage in southern B.C. The only trophies recovered are prized cougar photos.

His customers gather early in the morning, and his guides rapidly fan out to seek out cat tracks. When tracks are found, his dogs are released. And when the baying of the hounds reaches a steady, wild pitch, Langton knows that a cougar is treed. Only then does the party follow the dogs' trail to find the treed cat. Once it's located, both the dogs and the photographers go to the uphill side of the tree. (If the cat chooses to flee, it usually jumps downhill.) Rarely are the photographers disappointed. "There's definitely something about having this big cat sit over your head in a wild situation, and it's free," Langton says.

Langton is not the first hunter of big cats to have changed his attitudes toward the killing of his prey. Jim Corbett, a famed tiger hunter in India in the 1920s, largely gave up killing his prey by the 1930s and traded his gun for a camera. In *The Man-Eaters of Kumaon,* he wrote of his change of heart:

> *Apart from the difference in cost between shooting with a camera and shooting with a rifle, and the beneficial effect it has on our rapidly decreasing stock of tigers, the taking of a good photograph gives far more pleasure to the sportsman than the acquisition of a trophy; and further, while the photograph is of interest to all lovers of wildlife, the trophy is only of interest to the individual who acquired it.*

COUGARS AS PETS

High in the Ozark Mountains of Arkansas lies a very special place. Within its 463 acres, the Turpentine Exotic Wildlife Ranch provides refuge to sixty large exotic cats, including fourteen cougars. For many of the cats, the ranch is their final home after years of neglect in the hands of unthinking humans who thought the animals would make cute and interesting pets.

"People buy them when they are cute and cuddly little things and then don't know what to do with them when they get to be great big adults," says Don Jackson, owner of the refuge. The ranch operates as a nonprofit foundation, existing on private donations. One of its biggest problems is that faced by most owners of exotic cats: the sheer cost of feeding the animals. An adult cougar will consume over 2,000 pounds of meat every year; the Turpentine Ranch goes through over 21,000 pounds of food *per month*.

Aside from the hefty food bills, most owners of pet cougars simply can't provide adequate caging or care for their animals. An animal that requires 300 square miles of territory in the wild will never be happy in a backyard cage. Michael W. Fox, vice-president of the Humane Society of the United States, says that exotic pets "are not biologically adapted to live with humans." If the animal gets sick, few veterinarians will touch it.

And all too often, when the animals escape, the result is disaster. In 1990, for example, a pet cougar attacked a two-year-old Ohio boy; when his grandmother came to the boy's rescue, she too was attacked. Animals that escape can also cause problems by interbreeding with wild species and diluting pure gene pools, competing with wild animals for food, and transmitting disease.

Sadly, in the United States it is usually legal to own a pet cougar if you comply with state and local laws. And many people think that whatever they have in their backyards is their own business. Rusty Pitch is an exotic-animal dealer in southern Missouri. "Yeah, I sell cougars," he says. "So what's the big deal—we all gotta make a buck."

The result of attitudes like Rusty's is a flourishing $100-million-a-year business in exotic animals, centered in the southeastern United States. The market opened in the late 1960s, when zoos began selling off their excess animals. Thirty years later, game farms, private game ranches, private collectors, and hunting preserves are snapping up exotic animals at an alarming pace. Many are destined for "canned hunts" in which the unfortunate animals are released on a large ranch only to be hunted down and killed by big-game hunters who have few scruples concerning the source of their trophies. Others end up as short-term status symbols for their owners. Most of the animals never reach adulthood.

In many cases, the animals are not even treated as living things, but rather as mere objects of amusement. The December 1992 issue of *Animal Finders' Guide,* a publication that caters to would-be owners of exotic pets, advertised live cougar kittens as "stocking stuffers."

The cougar has suffered more than other animals as an exotic pet. Because it's relatively common, and native to North America, the price tag is relatively low: An adult cougar can be purchased for about $500, as opposed to $5,000 for a snow leopard.

Ron Sellton is a guide and outfitter in Idaho who owned a pet cougar for three years. "I shot its mother and then felt sorry for the little thing," he says. But he had troubles right away. "When a house cat sharpens its claws, it can ruin your couch," he says. "When my cougar did the same thing, it ruined my house." He also had problems with providing food for the rapidly growing kitten and with keeping it amused. "It didn't want to be a pet, it always wanted to get out." He finally gave the animal to a game farm. Ron's advice for those thinking of a cougar as a pet? "Forget it. The cat will never be happy and neither will you. Get a dog instead."

THE
EASTERN
COUGAR

▼▼▼

GOING
OR GONE?

I n May 1990, Robert Noble looked out the window of his brother's woodworking shop in Waasis, New Brunswick, and gasped. In the field nearby stood what Noble thought was a wild cougar, an animal supposedly extinct in the area for over half a century. "It gave me the chills," he said. He ran next door and borrowed a video recorder and photographed the animal as it prowled along the edge of the woods. The result is a fuzzy, seven-minute film that created a storm of controversy among biologists. Canadian biologist C. G. van Zyll de Jong doubts that the star of the film is a cougar; American biologist Jay Tischendorf believes that it is. Analysis by police film experts revealed that the cat was 20 to 26 inches long, qualifying it either as a very young cougar or a very large house cat. If the cat actually was a wild cougar, the film is a rare record of one of the most endangered animals in North America, the eastern cougar.

HISTORY OF THE EASTERN COUGAR

Taxonomists list twenty-seven different subspecies of cougars, fifteen of which live in North America. The various subspecies, according to E. A. Goldman, "are based on combinations of characters, including size, color, and details of cranial and dental structure that prevail in areas over which environmental conditions

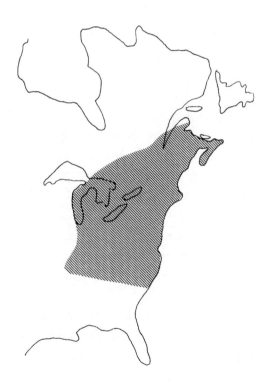

HISTORIC RANGE OF
THE EASTERN COUGAR

tend to be uniform." Of all these subspecies, the most problematic is *Felis concolor couguar,* the eastern cougar. The cat is a feline oxymoron, for although it's listed as endangered in both Canada and the United States, it may no longer even exist.

The eastern cougar's western neighbor, *F. c. schorgeri,* is believed by many authorities to have been extinct since 1930, although the U.S. Fish and Wildlife Service classes it as a Category 2 species, one step below endangered, due to a lack of documented evidence of its existence. Its southern cousin, the Florida panther, *F. c. coryi,* is barely clinging to survival in the swamps of Florida.

The eastern cougar was first labeled the *Cougar de Pensilvanie* by Count Buffon in 1776. It was renamed *Felis couguar* in 1792, then dropped to its current subspecies status in 1929. It can be distinguished from other cougar subspecies only by skull measurements.

Widespread persecution of the cougar led to its early demise from many parts of eastern North America by 1900. A mid-1800s report stated that the big cat was "nearly exterminated in our Atlantic States." The last cougar in Massachusetts was shot in 1841. Vermont's last big cat suffered the same fate in 1881. The last cougar recorded in the state of New York was shot by a bounty hunter in 1890. (In 1991, there was an ill-conceived plan to reintroduce cougars to the state of New York. A group of residents on Fire Island in Long Island Sound announced plans to introduce "thirty breeding pairs" of cougars in order to control the deer on the island. Few of the plan's proponents seemed to have done their homework. Cougars are polygamous animals; there is no such thing as a breeding pair. And the island might be able to sustain one cougar, but certainly not sixty. The plan was quietly dropped shortly after it was announced.)

In the 1930s, a Vermont newspaper offered a $1,000 reward for any cougar taken within the state. The reward was never collected. The eastern cougar was gone.

Or was it? In the 1940s, a new spate of eastern cougar sighting reports began to trickle in to wildlife officials, and a group of diehard eastern cougar supporters emerged.

THE EASTERN COUGAR
IN CANADA

The undisputed champion of the eastern cougar was the late Bruce Wright, director of the Northeastern Wildlife Station of the University of New Brunswick. Wright was the author of numerous articles and two books supporting the existence of the animal. Prior to Wright's investigations, the last verified sighting in eastern Canada was in 1938 along the Maine border. The animal was shot and is now on display in New Brunswick's provincial museum in Saint John. The largest number of eastern cougar sightings in Canada since the turn of the century came in 1948, following a widely read article by Wright in *Field & Stream*.

In 1953, Wright estimated that a population of thirty-three cougars still existed in New Brunswick. His method was adapted from a census technique that used the number of cougars killed in an area to determine the entire population. Wright substituted sightings for kills in the formula, and his method was widely criticized. Even the prestigious Committee on the Status of Endangered Wildlife in Canada (COSEWIC) commented in its *Status Report on the Eastern Cougar in Canada:* "Not much reliance can therefore be placed on Wright's estimate." It's perhaps fortunate that Wright didn't live to suffer this rejection; he died three years before the report's publication.

However, doubters of the animal's existence slowly began to note the accumulating numbers of eastern cougar sightings.

Although the last verified cougar shot in Ontario was taken in 1908, seasoned Canadian naturalist R. D. Lawrence found cougar tracks near Hearst, Ontario, in 1954, and actually sighted cougars in central Ontario in 1961 and 1969. He hasn't spotted a wild cougar in eastern Canada since. Then, in 1973, a cougar was shot near the Manitoba-Ontario border. Although some of these animals may have been captive cougars released into the wild, the sheer number of similar reports impressed the authorities.

After much debate, the eastern cougar was added to the endangered species list in the United States in 1973, and to Canada's endangered list in 1978. It's also listed in Appendix I of the Convention on International Trade in Endangered Species (CITES), which disallows the international trade in the animal or its parts among signatory countries.

The Canadian status report extrapolated predator/prey ratios from cougar studies in Idaho and commented that, theoretically, there were enough deer in New Brunswick to support a cougar population of about one hundred forty to two hundred fifty individuals.

Biologist Jay Tischendorf, a researcher with the American Ecological Research Institute in Colorado, once made the following comment on the survival ability of the Florida panther:

> *If they've been able to hold on for three or four centuries down in those fairly marginal swamp habitats, I think there is great evidence that, up in the northeast, in New Brunswick especially, the cats could continue to hold on as well.*

Indeed, in 1993, over ninety cougar sightings were reported in Nova Scotia and New Brunswick.

The 1978 working status report by the Committee on the Status of Endangered Wildlife in Canada recommended that "the existence of an eastern population of the cougar be confirmed and documented by the live-capture of one or more animals."

Almost twenty years later, no such confirmation yet exists.

➤ THE EASTERN COUGAR IN ➤ THE UNITED STATES

In October 1994, Rick Hedders saw a ghost. He was hunting deer in upstate New York when a large cat bounded out of the trees. "I stared at this thing and thought, 'This isn't supposed to be here,'" he says. He looked away for a few seconds to call his dogs and the cat disappeared. "I'm sure it was a cougar," he says. "Nothing around here is that big."

In the United States, reports of eastern cougars have been continuous from the 1940s to the present. Most sightings are similar to the one described above: a quick glimpse of a big cat. Few observers have had the time to take a photograph. Even fewer have thought later to look for tracks.

One way to measure the viability of cougar habitat is to look at the range of the cat's prime prey, the deer. Before Europeans landed in North America, an estimated thirty-four million white-tailed deer existed on the continent. Overhunting by humans, especially in the late 1800s, exterminated 98 percent of the deer population.

In 1953, Roger Tory Peterson and British naturalist James Fisher made an epic thirty-thousand-mile trip around North America. Their jaunt was chronicled in the classic *Wild America,* in which Peterson wrote, "A few mountain lions, even in this modern era, would not be a bad idea," adding that the "half-starved" deer of the southeastern United States would benefit from predation. His comments were remarkably prophetic.

When game laws began to protect the deer in the 1960s, the animal rebounded with a vengeance. Today's estimate for the continental deer population is about twenty million. And now, with no predators to maintain a natural balance, many of the southeastern states are overrun with deer. In 1994, the state of Virginia reported that it had over a million white-tailed deer, many of which were doomed to starvation. Such a strong deer population might well support a remnant population of cougars, especially in preserved areas such as national parks.

The highest number of eastern cougar (or eastern panther, as it is often called in the United States) sightings in any American national park has come from Great Smoky Mountains National Park. The last verified sighting in the Smokies was in 1920, when a cougar was killed near Fontana Village in North Carolina. But sightings have continued at the rate of about ten per year. In 1976 verified cougar hair samples were found in the park. In Tennessee a number of reports have come from the Greenbrier and Cosby areas, and a few from Cades Cove. In North Carolina, Cataloochee has been the location of many reported sightings. Most have been of single cats, but tantalizing reports of an adult with kittens have been noted in two different areas. However, Stuart Coleman, a resource management specialist for the park, states that "many people report black panthers, when ours are tawny." He notes that "we have no pug marks, no scats, no reliable photographs," and the official viewpoint of park officials is that all reports are either spurious or of captive cougars released to the wild. When biologists tried setting out scent baits near Cades Cove Visitor Center in an attempt to settle the issue, not one cougar was attracted.

Pennsylvania, whose last cougar was officially shot in 1891, has also had a continuous deer population. Numerous cougar sightings have been reported since 1900, and a specimen was shot in 1969.

Deer were scarce in the Appalachians of North Carolina by the late 1800s. Efforts to restore the population escalated with the establishment of the Pisgah Game Preserve and Pisgah National Forest, formerly parts of the vast Vanderbilt estate. Several reports exist of cougars shot in the mountainous regions of North Carolina, the most recent coming in 1981. In addition, the extensive swamp areas of the state may contain a hidden cougar population, for human penetration of the swamps is quite rare even today.

In West Virginia, strong deer populations have existed in the Jefferson–George Washington–Monongahela National Forests. Both cougar tracks and scat were found in these areas in 1981.

In September 1994, three cougars were spotted strolling through the woods near Craftsbury, Vermont. Scat was collected from the site and sent to the National Fish and Wildlife Forensics Laboratory in Ashland, Oregon. The laboratory confirmed the presence of cougar hairs in the scat, identifying them as foot hairs. The confirmation came as exciting news for the Friends of the Eastern Panther, a group that has promoted the belief in eastern cougars' existence for many years.

According to the group, "reliable sightings have now become so numerous that they no longer constitute 'news.'" Its members believe that a small, viable breeding population of eastern cougars exists in the northeastern United States and southeastern Canada and "that it is highly probable that these animals are descendants of the original stock present when the first Europeans came to North America." According to Ted Reed, a retired businessman and founder of the group, they believe "the animal was never extinct in the Northeast, but survived in small numbers in certain parts of New Brunswick and Maine. We believe these numbers have significantly increased over the last twenty to thirty years."

The organization has recommended the preservation of cougar habitat via the establishment of an international panther range in New Brunswick and Maine, and via the westward extension of Fundy National Park in New Brunswick. However, when the group sponsored a two-week cougar survey in southern New Brunswick in 1992, no signs of cougars were found.

The big question is whether any of the reported eastern cougar sightings in the past few decades have been of wild cougars, or have merely been of captive cougars released into the wild. It's also questionable whether many people can even identify a cougar. A recent study in British Columbia revealed that animals misidentified as cougars included a large dog, a house cat, two coyotes, and a small child. And single sightings do little to answer the question of whether a viable cougar population still exists in eastern North America. As Craig McLaughlin, a Maine biologist, has stated, "Unless we see evidence of breeding, it would be premature to say that we have a viable population here."

Rainer Brocke, professor of Wildlife Management at the State University of New York, believes that all sightings of cougars in the East are either misidentifications (95 percent) or of captive animals released to the wild (5 percent). He states firmly that "I would stake my life that there is no viable breeding population of panthers in northeastern United States or southeastern Canada."

The 1970 edition of the authoritative International Union for the Conservation of Nature (IUCN) *Red Book* was equally confident in its assessment of the eastern cougar: "This race has been extinct in the United States since the end of the last century."

In 1982, the U.S. Fish and Wildlife Service put together an Eastern Cougar Recovery Plan, with the prime goal of finding or establishing "at least three self-sustaining populations" of eastern cougars.

The service carried out a comprehensive study in Georgia, South Carolina, North Carolina, Tennessee, and Virginia from 1978 to 1983 to determine once and for all whether the eastern cougar still existed in those areas. After five years of intensive searching, no conclusive evidence of cougars was found.

Today, the view of the U.S. Fish and Wildlife Service is that the eastern cougar "does not exist as a breeding species east of the Mississippi."

The eastern ghost cat has probably vanished forever.

THE
FLORIDA
PANTHER

▼▼▼

NOWHERE
TO RUN

▶ HISTORY OF THE
▶ FLORIDA PANTHER

At one time, the Florida panther (a subspecies of cougar known to scientists as *Felis concolor coryi*) ranged from Florida north through Georgia, Mississippi, Alabama, Arkansas, Louisiana, and parts of Tennessee and South Carolina. The first European to spot one appears to have been the Spanish explorer Álvar Núñez Cabeza de Vaca, who reported seeing a cougar in 1513 near the Everglades.

THE SWAMP COUNTRY
OF SOUTHERN FLORIDA
IS THE FINAL HABITAT
OF THE FLORIDA
PANTHER.
(COURTESY EVERGLADES
NATIONAL PARK)

))))

It's interesting that almost exactly the same range was once inhabited by the red wolf, a small wolf species, which has now completely disappeared in the wild. Today, the Florida panther still exists in the wild, but barely.

The cat was originally labeled *Felis concolor floridana* by naturalist and hunter Charles B. Cory in 1896. However, it was soon pointed out that *F. floridana* was already the name used for the local race of bobcat, and so the panther's Latin name was changed in 1929.

The Florida panther is a medium-sized cougar, with males ranging from 100 to 150 pounds, and females from 50 to 100. Many animals captured in recent years have been at the low ends of these ranges due to various ailments. The panther has relatively short fur compared to the plush coat of other cougar subspecies, and has distinctive white flecks around its head, neck, and shoulders. It survived on deer, hogs, and raccoons in the southeastern corner of the United States for centuries with few natural enemies. But then came humans.

One of the earliest developers of southern Florida was Henry Flagler, a partner of John D. Rockefeller, who built a number of hotels in Florida in the late 1800s. In 1882, he stated that his aim was "to provide accommodations for the class of people…who come here to enjoy the climate, have plenty of money, but could find no satisfactory way of spending it." Flagler was also responsible for pushing the eastern rail lines south to his beloved hot spot. By 1896, the railroad had reached Miami, and the push began to drain the swampy lands south of Lake Okeechobee. Soon the wild habitat of southern Florida was changed forever, as ever-increasing hordes of winter-chilled people fled south to the Sunshine State.

By the 1920s, the panther had disappeared from much of its northern range, as hunters and ranchers had relentlessly destroyed both the animal and its habitat. At one point, the state of Florida even placed a bounty on the panthers, in an attempt to preserve the state's small deer population. Then the land developers arrived, plowing up vast tracks of the southeastern United States for citrus groves and subdivisions.

The establishment of Everglades National Park in 1947 almost came too late, for many species in southern Florida had already shown drastic declines. For example, by 1950, 98 percent of the area's alligator population had been exterminated. The park contains over one million acres, and only part of it is suitable as panther habitat.

The first warnings about the panther's very survival came a few years later. In 1958, the animal became protected by state law, and in 1967, the Florida panther was added to the first endangered species list in the United States. It's also now listed under Appendix I of the Convention on International Trade in Endangered Species (CITES), theoretically giving it protection from international trade.

However, international trade was the least of the panther's problems. When Florida State Highway 84 (now Interstate 75) was built

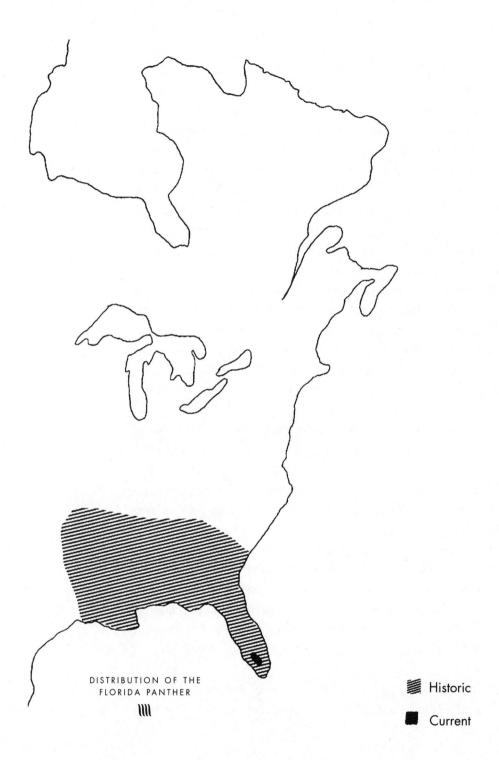

DISTRIBUTION OF THE
FLORIDA PANTHER

////

▨ Historic

■ Current

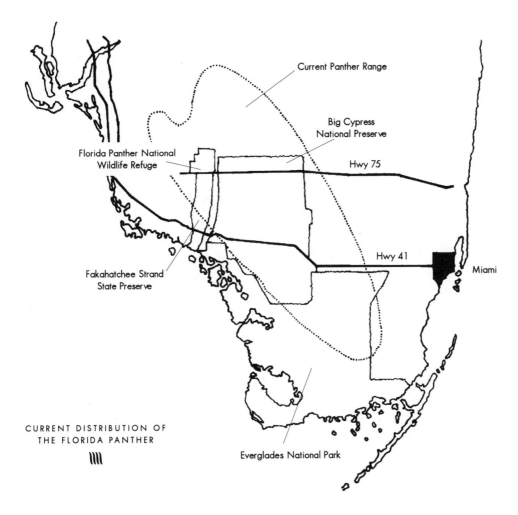

Current Panther Range

Big Cypress
National Preserve

Florida Panther National
Wildlife Refuge

Hwy 75

Fakahatchee Strand
State Preserve

Hwy 41

Miami

CURRENT DISTRIBUTION OF
THE FLORIDA PANTHER

Everglades National Park

right through the heart of panther country, a growing number of
cats died as a result of collisions with cars.

By the early 1970s, the Florida panther was gone from three-
quarters of its historic range, and could be found only in the mix of
mangrove swamps and grassy wetlands at the southern tip of
Florida. As state panther biologist Dave Maehr has noted, "The
panther isn't truly a swamp animal. In fact, they disdain swamps as
such. They stay out of them as much as they can." But this is where
humans have pushed them. The core of the remaining habitat was
only a half-hour drive west of the Miami city limits.

Unfortunately, much of that area was a popular site for deer hunting, and off-road vehicles and hunting dogs swarmed through the swamps on a regular basis. Subdivisions began creeping closer as swamps were drained and filled to house the flood of emigrants to Florida. The panther was being pushed into a smaller and smaller range.

➤ CONSERVATION EFFORTS FOR
➤ THE FLORIDA PANTHER

In 1973, the World Wildlife Fund brought in famed tracker Roy McBride to confirm that there were still some panthers left in the wild. McBride, probably the only bounty hunter to possess a college degree in biology, was the same man brought in by federal biologists to seek out the last Mexican wolves. His trained cougar hounds (lovingly described as his "professors of pantherology") found a small number of panthers hiding in the remote swamps of southern Florida, and the race began to save them. It was estimated at the time that only thirty to fifty panthers remained.

By 1981, the U.S. Fish and Wildlife Service had put together a recovery plan for the Florida panther. The plan detailed four major steps necessary for the panther's conservation: provision and conservation of habitat, monitoring of existing panthers by radiotracking, reestablishment of historic populations, and a public education program.

In 1982, the Everglades was recognized as an International Biosphere Reserve and a World Heritage Site, and world attention was focused on the unique animal life of southern Florida. (Florida today has more threatened and endangered species than any other jurisdiction in North America.) That same year, the Florida panther was declared the state animal.

To preserve the unique nature of the Everglades, Florida governor Bob Graham and seventeen major conservation groups announced a Save the Everglades campaign. The governor vowed:

"By the year 2000 the Everglades will look and function more like they did at the turn of the century."

As part of the program, lands cleared for agriculture were allowed to return to their wild state and some roads were rerouted to reduce the numbers of animals killed while attempting to cross the highways. Between 1980 and 1986, twelve panthers were struck by vehicles. Ten of the rare animals died.

The Florida Department of Transportation spent $25 million building thirty-six underpasses under a lethal stretch of I-75, the "Alligator Alley." It promised to spend an additional $4.5 million erecting a ten-foot-high chain-link fence to line the highway in an all-out bid to prevent additional panther deaths. (A similar fence along the Trans-Canada Highway through Alberta's Banff National Park has proved to be very successful in decreasing the number of animals killed along the busy stretch of road.)

A TEAM OF BIOLOGISTS ADMINISTERS TO A TRANQUILIZED FLORIDA PANTHER.
(DENNIS JORDAN, U.S. FISH & WILDLIFE SERVICE)

Along the Tamiami (Tampa-Miami) Trail, an east-west highway that runs along the northern edge of the Everglades, a series of signs was erected that mimicked the Burma Shave highway signs of the past. But their message was deadly serious: ENTERING PANTHER HABITAT...LESS THAN 30 REMAINING...PLEASE DRIVE CAREFULLY. Unfortunately, the panther was painted on the signs in black, leading many people to believe the actual cats were the same color.

The Florida Game and Fresh Water Fish Commission limited the use of all-terrain vehicles and hunting dogs in panther habitat, and closed deer hunting completely in the Fakahatchee Strand, a dense swamp of matted cypress, palms, and oaks north of the Everglades.

BIOLOGISTS MUST USE SPECIAL SWAMP BUGGIES TO TRACK THE FLORIDA PANTHER. (DENNIS JORDAN, U.S. FISH & WILDLIFE SERVICE)

IIII

Speed limits on roads in the panther's habitat were reduced to thirty miles per hour, and state troopers were instructed to be even less lenient than usual.

Workshops were held to help biologists share the results of their

panther research. Every little bit of new knowledge about the panther made its future a little bit brighter.

In a 1988 experiment, seven cougars from Texas were released north of the Osceola National Forest and were closely monitored. Within a year, three had died. One was found floating in the Suwanee River. Two were shot by hunters. The rest had strayed too close to civilization for the biologists' comfort, and evidence suggested that the panthers' terrified reaction to the hunters and their dogs caused the cats to scatter. The survivors were captured and quietly shipped back home.

In 1989, a special thirty-thousand-acre Florida Panther Refuge was set up adjacent to the Big Cypress National Preserve in order to provide more habitat for panthers. The refuge also protects a number of other endangered animals, such as the eastern indigo snake, snail kite, and peregrine falcon.

More panther habitat was saved with the addition of over eighty thousand acres to the Big Cypress National Preserve and of over a hundred thousand acres to Everglades National Park.

The U.S. Fish and Wildlife Service gathered all known data on the Florida panther in 1989 and fed it into a computer for a prognosis of the cat's future. The output was forbidding. Without additional human help, the panther would be extinct within twenty-five to forty years.

By 1991, twenty panthers were sporting radio collars. Upon capture, each cat was given vitamins, vaccines, and dewormers. Samples of blood, tissue, and sperm were taken for analysis at the National Zoo and the National Cancer Institute, both in Washington, D.C. The results were shocking. The tiny remnant population was dangerously inbred, and its future looked grim. The cats had few choices when it came to mating, and so sisters mated with brothers and mothers with sons. For most species, a minimum of fifty to five hundred individuals is necessary to ensure maximum genetic diversity. By 1991, it was estimated that only twenty-five to thirty Florida panthers remained.

Isolated populations of animals can suffer from two genetic problems: *inbreeding* and *loss of genetic variability*. Inbreeding is the breeding of closely related animals, and often manifests itself generations later through abnormal sperm, decreasing fertility, and increased mortality. A classic case of inbreeding has been found among the lions in Tanzania's Ngorongoro Crater. Isolated by high walls and maintained by high numbers of game, the lions of Ngorongoro have been found to have all descended from only fifteen individuals. More than half of the sperm tested from the Ngorongoro lions has been found to be abnormal, containing twice the number of abnormalities in lions from the adjacent Serengeti Plain.

Stephen J. O'Brien, a geneticist with the National Cancer Institute, has described the vicious progression of inbreeding: "As they begin to inbreed, congenital defects appear, both physical and reproductive. Often abnormal sperm increase; infertility rises; the birthrate falls. Most perilous in the long run, each animal's immune system is weakened." A weak immune system makes an animal extremely susceptible to bacteria, viruses, and parasites.

Genetic variability refers to the variability in qualities such as height, weight, or resistance to disease within animals in a species. It's the latter that's crucial: Without sufficient variation in resistance, a new disease can wipe out an entire species.

Biologists quickly found that the Florida panther both was inbred and had low genetic variability. Analysis showed that the panther was losing about 7 percent of its genetic diversity with each generation. The panthers had a unique kink at the end of the tail and a contrary cowlick of fur along the back, thought by many biologists to be badges of inbreeding. The problems caused by inbreeding also showed up in more insidious ways. Most of the males of the population were *cryptorchids*—animals with only one descended testicle in the scrotum. Over 90 percent of the males were found to have abnormal sperm. Melody Roelke, the state panther veterinarian, declared desperately at one point, "If it gets any worse, they won't procreate, period."

In addition, a third of the cats had heart murmurs, and many had actual holes in their heart walls. A third of cats captured had FIV, feline immunodeficiency virus. Half of the cats had feline calicivirus, an upper respiratory ailment. The majority of the panthers had feline panleukopenia, a highly contagious viral disease that's often called feline distemper. Heavy hookworm infestations in many of the panthers had led to chronic anemia and weight loss. The carcass of one poor panther examined in 1985 harbored 744 hookworms.

To make matters even worse, in 1991, an autopsy of the last known female panther in the Everglades revealed unusually high levels of mercury in her blood. Two other cats in the Everglades also died later with high blood levels of the toxin. The mercury was thought to have an aquatic source and to have been ingested by fish. The fish were then eaten by raccoons, and the raccoons were in turn eaten by panthers. All too often, it's the major predators at the top of the food chain that pay the ultimate price. The wild panthers were indeed in big trouble.

As a last resort, the recovery biologists decided to remove some cats from the wild to start a captive breeding program. Melody Roelke referred to the program as an "insurance policy" for the future. However, the recovery team failed to recognize the power of the animal rights lobbies that have mushroomed in the United States since the 1960s. And very quickly, the animal rights movement made its anger known.

The protesters were led by Gainesville animal rights activist Holly Jensen, a community nurse who shook up the whole panther conservation effort. Jensen claimed that as "a symbol of wild Florida," the panthers should remain in the wild and nature should be allowed to take its course. It was a noble stand, but it failed to acknowledge the fact that the panthers were not dying from natural causes, but rather due to the activities of humans.

However, she and her supporters gained the backing of the powerful Fund for Animals, a New York–based organization led by self-styled "professional curmudgeon" Cleveland Amory. In 1991, the fund sued the U.S. Fish and Wildlife Service on the grounds that an adequate environmental impact statement had not been filed for the proposed panther breeding program. They asserted that the service had violated both the National Environmental Policy Act and the Endangered Species Act.

The suit was quietly settled out of court, with the U.S. Fish and Wildlife Service agreeing to file a Supplemental Environmental Assessment to address the protesters' concerns. Meanwhile, precious time had been lost. During the legal wrangling, at least eleven cats died, primarily from collisions with cars.

In 1991, six kittens were removed from the wild to start the captive breeding program. The program got off to a bad start when one of the kittens was found to have a defective heart valve. It was removed from the program and sent to the Wildlife Research Laboratory near Gainesville for emergency treatment.

The original plan was to remove one or two adult panther pairs and up to six kittens annually in order to build up a captive population. The first two adult cats to enter the program were accident victims, rescued by biologists—who prefer to disturb the wild adult population as little as possible—after being hit by cars. The ultimate goal was a captive colony of 130 panthers by the year 2000.

The first captive cats were held on the White Oak Plantation, a 500-acre conservation center owned by Howard Gilman, owner of Gilman Paper Company. The plantation sits near the border between Florida and Georgia, and currently holds five Florida panthers. Incidentally, the plantation also holds a dance studio where Mikhail Baryshnikov once danced: Baryshnikov dancing to save the arts and Gilman striving to save the panthers, a beautiful dual image of hope. Two panthers are also held at the Lowry Park Zoological Garden in Tampa, and two others at the Jacksonville Zoo.

After years of controversy, it was decided that the captive breeding effort would not produce results fast enough to save the Florida panther. Biologists therefore chose not to disturb the wild cats by removing more individuals into captivity. Instead, it was decided to add some new blood to the population by importing cougars from Texas. The current plan, much debated and finally approved in 1994, was to capture up to eight Texas cougars and release them, likely two at a time, into the panther habitat of southern Florida. The cats were captured under contract by Roy McBride and are radio-collared for easy monitoring of their progress. As of January

1996, twenty-six Texas cougars have been relocated to Florida. So far, eighteen have survived.

The plan, described as a "genetic restoration" move by Florida biologists, has also met with a great deal of controversy. The Texas cougars are a different subspecies altogether from the Florida panthers, and some purists are opposed to the project as just another example of human manipulation of nature.

➤ THE FUTURE OF THE
➤ FLORIDA PANTHER

Today, the remnant wild panther population occupies less than 1 percent of the subspecies' original range. About half of all known wild Florida panthers live on private lands north of the Everglades and south of Lake Okeechobee, where they must compete for space with both cattle and humans.

Unfortunately, the push for additional development of southern Florida continues to pose many threats to the panther. Large-scale agricultural operations, with their attendant use of pesticides and fertilizers, have covered much of the land; the extensive network of artificial canals and ditches hinders the movements of both panthers and prey.

Most of southern Florida has always had low densities of deer due to the poor quality of the habitat—known for soggy ground conditions and high parasite levels. Biologists have experimented with supplementing the natural food supplies of the panthers by releasing sterilized wild hogs. The experiment has met with little success, with alligators and humans taking more hogs than the panthers.

Chris Belden, a U.S. Fish and Wildlife Service biologist with the panther recovery team, worked for four years in panther country before spotting one. One of the many new threats he has worried about is oil development. "Oil has been found in the Big Cypress

[National Preserve]," he says. "Twenty-five oil wells are there right now, with more planned…it is the access roads to them that cause the great danger." There's also a growing demand for additional subdivisions, citrus groves, and sugarcane fields.

If captive breeding is eventually successful, or if the imported Texas cats mate with their Florida cousins, potential reintroduction sites for the Florida panther include the Osceola National Forest, Apalachicola National Forest, and Big Ben Coast in Florida, as well as the Okefenokee National Wildlife Refuge in Georgia. Recently, the Pinhook Swamp was given legal protection, providing an important habitat link between the Osceola National Forest and the Okefenokee National Wildlife Refuge. The recovery team ultimately hopes to achieve three viable, self-sustaining populations within the historic range of the animal.

Historically, reintroductions of endangered species have not met with great success. Of 146 international reintroduction programs monitored by the U.S. National Zoo in Washington, D.C., only 11 percent have succeeded. Recently, the U.S. Fish and Wildlife Service announced that half of the reintroductions attempted in the United States have ended in failure. One of the best known was the $1.5 million attempt to reintroduce whooping cranes to the Gray's Lake area in Idaho. After fourteen years, not a single crane has produced offspring. To date, the direct costs of the Florida panther recovery program have exceeded $2 million.

Even if the captive panther breeding program succeeds, will there be room for the big cats in Florida? Alan Lieberman of the San Diego Zoo has pointed out that "there is no point in carefully saving, breeding, and returning creatures to the wild if the original cause of their demise is still present." And as Holly Jensen says, "What about saving habitat?…What you'll end up with are caged cats and nowhere to put them."

To be successful, reintroductions must meet two crucial criteria. There must be sufficient habitat for the reintroduced species, and there must be little possibility of interference from human activities. Unfortunately, southern Florida receives poor marks in both areas, having one of the highest growth rates in all of North America, with almost a thousand new residents arriving daily. The area already contains over five million people and is host to millions of tourists each year. And the Miami International Airport is among the busiest airports on the continent. The demand for additional housing subdivisions and resort developments is intense, and much of the privately owned habitat will be gone within a few years.

Given the booming population of Florida, it's unlikely that a large population of panthers will ever again roam the state. Small numbers may cling to survival in the most remote swamps, and perhaps a small population will successfully hide within the larger wildlife preserves. But they'll be mere shadows of the former numbers, a sad remnant. Ghosts in a swamp.

THE
FUTURE
OF THE COUGAR

▼▼▼

P erhaps because the cougar is rarely seen by humans, and has none of the lengthy mythology of such animals as the wolf, few voices have been raised for its conservation—until recently. Richard M. Hopper, chief of the Wildlife Research Unit at the Colorado Division of Wildlife, notes that "observation of this animal in the wild by the general public is a rarity. This has characterized the species as being mysterious and largely misunderstood." A great deal of cougar research over the past two decades is slowly changing that.

COUGAR RESEARCH

For years, the classic text on cougars was Stanley Young and E. A. Goldman's *The Puma: Mysterious American Cat*, published in 1946. Almost three decades later, the amount of information on cougars had not expanded to any degree; a *New Mexico Wildlife* article on the cougar was aptly entitled "*Felis concolor,* Our Big and Mysterious Cat." Only recently has this label begun to be erased, as biologists turn their attention to the cougar. With the elimination of the wolf and the grizzly from most parts of this continent, the dominant remaining predator is the cougar.

The first step in conserving the cougar is understanding its basic biology. In the 1930s, Frank Hibben was the first biologist to study cougars using a microscope instead of a gun barrel. He followed cougar hunters in Arizona and New Mexico and analyzed stomach contents of the dead cougars. Hibben found that deer comprised the main portion of the cats' diet, and that most of the deer were not prime, mature specimens. Hibben was one of the first to conceive of tracking the cats by the use of ear tags, but he dropped the idea, fearing it would "raise too much opposition with cattle and game interests."

In the 1940s, biologist Stanley Young gathered information from federal trappers and bounty hunters to write his book. The era of scientific cougar field research had not yet begun.

The 1950s and early 1960s saw W. Leslie Robinette carrying out some of the first field studies in Utah and Nevada, although he still used the stomach contents of dead cougars to reveal their eating habits.

Studies of live wild cougars were finally launched in the 1960s with the work of Maurice Hornocker. A graduate of the University of British Columbia and the University of Montana, Hornocker did grizzly research with the famed Craighead brothers before turning his attention to the little-known cougar.

He began in Montana in 1963, radio-collaring cougars in the high western foothills, but switched to central Idaho the next year after most of his Montana cats were shot by hunters. For ten years, Hornocker and his associates tracked the big cats through the wild Idaho Primitive Area (now called the Frank Church River of No Return Wilderness), discovering much of what we know today about basic cougar biology. His work was the prime impetus for the reclassification of the cougar in most areas from varmint to big-game animal, a major move for cougar conservation.

Although Hornocker has stated that "as a scientist, I must view my subject in an objective, 'scientific' manner," there is no question that his work has ingrained in him a love and respect for big cats.

In 1984, the New Mexico Department of Game and Fish asked Hornocker to perform a ten-year study of their cougar population. He hired the husband-and-wife team of Ken Logan and Linda Sweanor, who have concentrated their efforts on the San Andres Mountains on the edge of the White Sands Missile Range. Their work is of great significance not only to cougar management, but also to wolf studies, for the White Sands Missile Range and the surrounding publically owned land is one of two potential reintroduction sites for the endangered Mexican wolf. What will the relationship be between these two great predators? Can the two coexist? Is there sufficient game for both? Only a long-term study such as the one just completed will help answer these questions.

In 1986, Hornocker turned his attention to Yellowstone National Park, another jurisdiction that's currently being repopulated with wolves. As recently as the 1920s, park officials regularly shot both cougars and wolves in a bid to benefit the park's other wildlife. Hornocker and his associates determined that a small population of eighteen adult cougars lived in the northern Yellowstone region, a discovery that surprised a number of the rangers who had worked in the park for years.

In recent years, Hornocker has worked with Russian biologists to save the highly endangered Siberian tiger. His many pursuits led him to leave the leadership of the Cooperative Wildlife Research Unit at the University of Idaho and found the nonprofit Hornocker Wildlife Research Institute to coordinate his wildlife studies around the world. Hornocker is currently directing a five-year study of the relationship between wolves and cougars in Montana's Glacier National Park.

Other American cougar researchers of note include John Seidensticker, who worked with Maurice Hornocker in Idaho; Harley Shaw, who followed the big cats in Arizona; and Fred Lindzey, who coordinated a long-term cougar project in Utah.

In Canada, the Sheep River cougar study in southern Alberta, begun in 1982, has been an outstanding source of data on Canadian cougars. For its first four years, the study was underwritten by the Alberta Fish and Wildlife Division. When project biologist Orval Pall was killed in a plane crash in 1986, Arc Associated Resource Consultants of Calgary was chosen to finish writing the study's final report. Arc's team of Martin Jalkotzy, Ralph Schmidt, and Ian Ross decided to continue the study, stating "we really believe in long-term research. Too often the funding stops after a few years just when the project gets rolling." With the financial aid of the World Wildlife Fund Canada, the Canadian Wildlife Federation, Shell Canada, and others, the Alberta Cougar Project is now the longest-running cougar study in North America.

One of the major findings of the study to date was that cougars were being overhunted within many of the hunting management units in Alberta. The World Wildlife Fund Canada has recommended that recreational hunting should not take over 10 percent of a cougar population in any one year. Alberta's own Fish and Wildlife Division recommends that "a maximum man-caused mortality rate of not more than 15 percent per year" be allowed. Jalkotzy and his associates were able to document seventeen instances of overhunting in specific areas between 1978 and 1989. In some cases, 20 percent of the estimated area cougar population was being shot each year. As a result of the team's studies, Alberta cougar hunting regulations were changed in 1990. (The documented overhunting of cougars is not unusual: In 1983, one researcher in western Montana found that 50 percent of his resident adult cougars were killed by hunters.)

In South America, both William Franklin and J. L. Yanez have studied the cougars of Chile's Patagonia region. They have found one of the densest concentrations of cougars anywhere; the cats subsist on young guanacos (wild llama-like animals) and European hares. Louise Emmons has followed cougars through the jungles of Peru to understand their food requirements, documenting such unusual cougar fare as lizards and bats.

According to the Mountain Lion Foundation, a pro-cougar lobby based in Sacramento, California, additional cougar research is still needed in the following areas: long-term behavior studies, population censuses, age statistics, habitat studies, and predator-prey relationships. Colorado biologist Allen E. Anderson has recommended that "research on the effects of sport hunting on specific puma populations" should receive top priority. There's also a massive need for research of all types in Mexico, and in Central and South America. And there's a pressing need for less intrusive research methods: In one 1983 survey of cougar studies, 10 percent of 115 monitored cougars died as a result of the studies themselves. Almost half of these were kittens killed by hounds. Recently, biologists in the Big Bend National Park in Texas have recommended the use of live traps instead of hunting dogs and tranquilizer darts to reduce the cougar mortality. The live traps are also much less expensive, averaging $81 per capture, compared to the $561 spent per capture using trained hounds.

➤PUBLIC EDUCATION

The second step in cougar conservation is presenting the information gained by research on the animal to the public. Mountain lion workshops have been held in Reno in 1976, in southern Utah in 1984, in Prescott, Arizona, in 1988, and in San Diego in 1996. A program teaching the public to recognize cougar tracks, signs, and scratches would go a long way toward garnering support for cougar conservation. The Sheep River cougar study in southern Alberta found that "the cougar in Alberta is poorly understood" and that "many people apparently do not know that cougars occur in Alberta." One of the study's many recommendations was the implementation of a public education program. The same recommendation could well be applied to every jurisdiction where the cougar still exists.

⟩Loss of Habitat

When Karl Borter came to the Cariboo country of central British Columbia in 1948, he occasionally saw cougars when he made his rounds checking his traplines. But the 1950s heralded the invasion of logging trucks into the pristine cedar rain forests, and the local wildlife retreated farther and farther into the mountains. Borter has not seen a cougar anywhere in the Cariboo since 1964.

By far the most significant risk faced by cougars today is loss of habitat. As Martin Jalkotzy says, "We're eating up the boreal foothills that are cougar habitat, and deer, elk, and moose habitat as well." Or as biologist Steven Herrero, of the University of Calgary, has stated bluntly, "You don't protect the animal, you protect the habitat."

And where man does invade cougar habitat, the cougar retreats. American biologist and cougar researcher F. G. van Dyke discovered that cougars selected home ranges that contained no recent logging areas and few or no sites with resident humans. He also found that they crossed well-maintained, hard-surfaced roads less frequently than smaller dirt roads. In a 1986 master's degree thesis at Utah State University, Dan Barnhurst recommended additional road closures in remote areas to help conserve cougars. "The potential impact on the cougar population should be considered in the environmental impact statement of any planned projects that include construction of new roads," he wrote.

Cougars also face more direct risks from humans and human activities. Of twenty-two cougars studied in southern Alberta between 1981 and 1988, 64 percent were shot by humans. Over half of the cougar deaths in one study in B.C.'s Kootenay district

were due to the animals being struck by cars. And cars are also the major killer of cougars in California. In one incident in Colorado, three juvenile cougars were killed by a train.

Clearly, there's a need for wild habitat free of humans and human activities in which the cougar and other large predators can live and hunt in freedom. Those who believe that our parks are the answer need to reconsider.

Most of our parks have been designed as playgrounds for people, with the inherent wildlife given little or no consideration. One of the conclusions of the First World Conference on National Parks, held in Seattle in 1962, was that "few of the world's parks are large enough to be in fact self-regulatory ecological units." Most parks are too small and too isolated to act as efficient reservoirs of large predators and their prey. Many are overrun with visitors: The national parks in the United States alone receive almost three hundred million visitors each year. And to make matters worse, many parks allow hunting, nullifying their status as true game preserves.

In Canada, the World Wildlife Fund Canada has recommended the establishment of large Carnivore Conservation Areas "to conserve viable, wild populations of large carnivores." It has recommended that the Rocky Mountain parks complex along the Alberta–British Columbia border be set aside as a conservation area rich in large predators, including both cougars and grizzlies. The area is now partly government-owned land, partly national parks, and partly provincial parks, necessitating a high degree of cooperation between federal and provincial authorities if a conservation area is to be established.

In the United States, a number of biologists have recommended establishing a linked set of parks, stretching down the rugged corridor from Glacier National Park south to New Mexico, as a potential preserve for large predators. Very few other blocks within the U.S. are large enough to be truly called wilderness or to efficiently act as safe refuges for large predators.

The idea has the enthusiastic support of cougar researchers. Larry Harris, a Florida cougar biologist, has stated that "our numerous, large wildlife sanctuaries must be made to function as a system, rather than being…islands." And cougar biologist Linda Sweanor believes that "to conserve populations of mountain lions over the long term, adequate habitats must be maintained in an effective patchwork composed of relatively large blocks of wildland reserves interconnected by dispersal corridors." Again, a great deal of interstate cooperation would be required.

Without dispersal corridors and the influx of transient cats, the survival of most small cougar populations is doubtful. Biologist Dr. Paul Beier once calculated minimum habitat requirements for cougars based on his work in California. He found that without immigration, for a viable breeding population (about fifty to one hundred cougars) to survive for 100 years, a minimum block of 620 square miles is required. Blocks this size of pure wilderness are almost nonexistent in the United States today.

Pioneer field biologist John Craighead once asked: "Is wilderness in the traditional sense an illusion at the end of the twentieth century?" For most of the United States, the tragic answer is yes.

➤ THE EFFECTS OF
➤ COUGAR HUNTING

Where cougar populations still exist, cougar hunting regulations must be fair and based on sound management practices.

One abuse of hunting regulations that still occurs in some areas is the "will-call" system, in which cougar licenses are not purchased until a cat is actually treed. By using this method, some hunters avoid having to purchase licenses, cheating the local wildlife departments out of urgently needed dollars. Sometimes the unfortunate cat is forced to wait treed for days until its killer arrives. It has been estimated that almost a third of all guided cougar hunts in Arizona are such will-call hunts. Cougar biologists recommend that all jurisdictions issue licenses early in the season and for a limited period of time to prevent this practice from continuing.

Some states, such as Idaho, allow a pursuit season in which cougars may not be hunted, but may be harassed by outfitters training their hounds. The purported nonconsumptive nature of pursuit seasons is often questioned. For example, the Alberta Fish and Wildlife Division does not allow pursuit seasons for the following reasons: "Young kittens may be captured and killed by hounds, ungulate kills made by cougars may be abandoned, and...continued harassment may induce physiological trauma." It can only be hoped that other jurisdictions will follow Alberta's example.

Some biologists have expressed concern about the number of cougar kittens killed by hunting dogs. One Utah researcher stated that "it is probable that in some areas, cub mortality from maulings and orphaning is as significant as adult harvest." And biologists

COUGAR MORTALITY IN MONTANA, 1993–1994

Class	Number of Cougars	Percentage of Total Mortality
Hunters	413	87
Road kill	16	4
Unknown	15	3
Damage control	11	2
Illegally killed	6	1
Nuisance control	4	1
Self-defense	4	1
Accidental snare	2	< 1
Trapping	2	< 1
Natural causes	2	< 1
Dogs	1	< 1
Train	1	< 1
	477	100

Source: Montana Department of Fish, Wildlife, and Parks

themselves have inadvertently caused kitten mortality when their tracking dogs have treed a mother cougar with kittens. In Maurice Hornocker's pioneer Idaho studies, three kittens were killed by dogs and one juvenile died when a tranquilizer dart punctured its lung.

THE PLACID DEMEANOR
OF A TREED COUGAR
(© LYN HANCOCK)

In addition to hunting deaths, a number of cougars have met their deaths by accidentally getting caught in traps set for other animals. Many lose toes or break legs trying to escape from the traps and, when found, are usually killed by the trapper. Few of these accidental catches are reported.

Wain Evans of the New Mexico Department of Game and Fish found in a review of that state's cougar management that "cougars killed by private trappers and hunters under depredation permits were frequently not reported."

It's common for supporters of sport hunting to vow that hunting keeps cougar populations healthy and manageable. However, there's no scientific evidence to support these contentions.

⮚ POACHING OF COUGARS

L ike most other predators, the cougar is also pursued to some degree by poachers. There's a small demand for cougar galls in the Far East, and there are always those who don't question the source of a stuffed trophy. The numbers of cats that are poached is, of course, difficult to assess. The Washington Department of Game estimated that in 1988, 32 of the 121 cougars killed in their state were killed illegally.

Luckily, the demand for illegal trophies is decreasing as the tolerance of North Americans for trophy hunting has declined.

⮚ THE COUGAR TODAY

D espite the many problems facing the cougar, recent years have seen a flurry of cougar sightings and cougar reports in the popular media.

Part of the explanation for the apparent increase in cougar num-

COUGARS KILLED BY SPORT HUNTERS, 1994–1995

State/Province	Cougar Harvest
Alberta	54
Arizona	215
British Columbia	543
Colorado	316
Idaho	328
Montana	604
Nevada	161
New Mexico	63
Oregon	144
Texas	99[1]
Utah	508[2]
Washington	177
Wyoming	77

1. Includes cougars taken by landowners and by hired private hunters
2. Includes cougars taken for depredation

bers is the increased number of humans moving into the cats' habitat and observing them for the first time. Today, there are few wilderness areas in North America that haven't been overwhelmed by hikers, hunters, loggers, or mountain bikers.

However, it's thought that part of the apparent increase in

cougar numbers since the 1960s is real—a pleasant by-product of improved public attitudes toward animals in general and predators in particular. According to Dr. Paul Beier, "cougar populations throughout the West probably increased during 1965–1980 as [virtually] each state and province changed the legal status of the cougar from bountied predator to game species." In one 1988 survey, biologists reported increased cougar numbers in British Columbia, California, Colorado, Nevada, Texas, and Wyoming.

In fact, in recent years a number of cougars have even stumbled into urban centers across North America. In 1989, one young cougar blundered into a brewery in New Westminster, British Columbia. In 1990, two cougars were spotted strolling along busy Interstate 5 near Sacramento. That same year, a young cougar shocked shoppers when it ambled through a busy Missoula parking lot. In 1991, a cougar sauntered into the parking lot of the Empress Hotel in Victoria, British Columbia. Like many other occupants of the structure, it could not find the exit ramp. It was escorted out under sedation by wildlife officials.

While these incidents may be mildly amusing, other tales of cougars entering cities have not had such happy endings. In August 1992, one young cougar made the mistake of following a stream valley right into the city of Denver. A dog promptly chased it up a tree, and the dog's owner called the police. Soon, the incident took on the proportions of a major news event, with firefighters, television crews, wildlife officers, and police arriving in force. The cat quietly watched the circus below it until it was darted; then it jumped down in a quick bid to escape. The police panicked and opened fire, and the unfortunate cougar was killed by dozens of shots. As a wise man once said, In the war between man and nature, nature seldom wins.

Although the western cougar population seems to be thriving, other races of cougar are not doing so well. Currently, the U.S. Fish and Wildlife Service recognizes three endangered subspecies of cougars: the eastern cougar, the Florida panther, and the Costa Rican puma *(Felis concolor costaricensis)*. All three are given protection under Appendix I of the Convention on International Trade

LEGAL STATUS OF THE COUGAR

State/Province	Status	State/Province	Status
Alberta	Game Animal	Nevada	Game Animal
Arizona	Game Animal	New Mexico	Game Animal
British Columbia	Game Animal	Oregon	Game Animal
California	Protected	Texas	Game Animal
Colorado	Game Animal	Utah	Game Animal
Florida	Protected	Washington	Game Animal
Idaho	Game Animal	Wyoming	Game Animal
Montana	Game Animal		

in Endangered Species (CITES). However, little cougar research has been undertaken throughout most of Central and South America, and it's very possible that other threatened subspecies exist.

Two other subspecies are listed as candidates for endangered status: the Wisconsin puma *(F. c. schorgeri)* and the delightfully named Yuma puma *(F. c. browni)*. However, many biologists believe that the Wisconsin puma is already extinct, and some biologists don't recognize either subspecies as separate. (The Wisconsin puma, for example, was subspeciated on the evidence of only three specimens found in Wisconsin, Minnesota, and Kansas—a very small database.)

CONCLUSION

The wolf, the grizzly, and the cougar. The great dog, the great bear, and the great cat, all pushed into the attics of the Earth by the spread of the greatest predator of all—humanity.

THE TWILIGHT WORLD
OF THE WILD COUGAR
(© LYN HANCOCK)

||||

Essayist David Quammen once wrote, "As we continue losing the large predators,…we'll lose something else too: the important spiritual influence that they have exerted…toward keeping us humble." And humble we should be, when faced with a great predator, as well as respectful of its right to survive.

We must not become complacent because the cougar's numbers appear to be increasing in many areas. We once said the same thing about the plains buffalo, passenger pigeon, giant anole, Alabama River snail, plains wolf, Merriam's elk, sea mink, Steller's sea cow, Atlantic gray whale, California grizzly, badlands bighorn, Carolina parakeet, Labrador duck, and great auk. All were once resident in North America. All are now gone forever.

May the cougar never join that list of shame.

APPENDIX

►Cougar Conservation
►Organizations

Mountain Lion Foundation, P.O. Box 1896, Sacramento, CA 95812

Friends of the Eastern Panther, P.O. Box 102, 41 Front Street, Exeter, NH 03888

►Other Conservation
►Organizations

Canadian Nature Federation, Suite 520, 1 Nicholas Street, Ottawa, Ontario K1N 7B7

Canadian Wildlife Federation, 2740 Queensview Drive, Ottawa, Ontario K2B 1A2

Conservation International, Suite 1000, 1015 18th Street N.W., Washington, DC 20036

Defenders of Wildlife, 1244 19th Street N.W., Washington, DC 20036

Friends of the Everglades, #2, 101 Westward Drive, Miami Springs, FL 33166

National Audubon Society, 700 Broadway, New York, NY 10003

National Wildlife Federation, 1400 16th Street N.W., Washington, DC 20036

Sierra Club, 730 Polk Street, San Francisco, CA 94109

Wildlife Conservation Society, Bronx, NY 10460

Wildlife Damage Review, P.O. Box 85218, Tucson, AZ 85754

Wilderness Society, 900 17th Street N.W., Washington, DC 20006

World Wildlife Fund, 1250 24th Street N.W., Washington, DC 20037

BIBLIOGRAPHY

Adamson, Joy. *Queen of Shaba*. London: Collins Harvill, 1980.

Alberta Fish and Wildlife Division. *Status of the Fish and Wildlife Resource in Alberta*. 1984. 49 pp.

Allen, Thomas B. *Vanishing Wildlife of North America*. Washington, D.C.: National Geographic Society, 1974.

Anderson, A. E. *A Critical Review of Literature on Puma* (Felis concolor). Denver: Colorado Division of Wildlife, 1983. 91 pp.

Atkins, Lynn. "Camera for Cougar." *B.C. Outdoors,* 48 (1), 1992: 51–53.

Audubon Society Field Guide to North American Mammals. New York: Alfred A. Knopf, 1980.

Bailey, Paul. "F.I.V. Positive." *Nature Canada,* 23 (3): 12–13.

Beasley, Conger, Jr. "Killing Coyotes." *Buzzworm,* 93 (1), 1993: 36–41.

Bergman, Charles. *Wild Echoes: Encounters with the Most Endangered Animals in North America*. New York: McGraw-Hill Publishing Company, 1989.

Bigony, Mary-Love. "Cat of Controversy." *Texas Parks & Wildlife*, April 1993: 1–10.

Booth, Cathy. "Miami Latina." *Reader's Digest,* 146 (874), 1995: 14–20.

Braun, Clait E., ed. *Mountain Lion–Human Interaction Symposium and Workshop*. Denver: Colorado Division of Wildlife, 1991. 114 pp.

Chase, Alston. "Wild Thing." *Countryside,* 2 (5), 1991: 108–109.

Conaway, James. "Eastern Wildlife—Bittersweet Success." *National Geographic*, 181 (2), 1992: 66–90.

Cougar. Ottawa: Canadian Wildlife Service, 1990. 4 pp.

"Cougar Counting." *B.C. Outdoors,* 47 (6), 1991: 25.

Cougar in British Columbia. Victoria: B.C. Ministry of the Environment, Wildlife Branch, 1988. 4 pp.

"Craftsbury Panthers: A Watershed Event." *Panther Prints,* Fall 1994: 1.

Cramond, Mike. *Big Game Hunting in the West*. Vancouver: Mitchell Press, Ltd., 1965.

Dutcher, Jim, and Karen McCall. *Cougar: Ghost of the Rockies*. San Francisco: Sierra Club Books, 1992.

Evans, Wain. *The Cougar in New Mexico: Biology, Status, Depredation of Livestock, and Management Recommendations*. Santa Fe: New Mexico Department of Game and Fish, 1983. 40 pp.

Fisher, Susan. "On the Cougar's Trail." *International Wildlife,* 23 (2), 1993: 29.

Franklin, William L. "Patagonia Puma: The Lord of Land's End." *National Geographic,* 179 (1), 1991: 102–113.

Garner, Joe. *Never a Time to Trust.* Nanaimo, B.C.: Cinnabar Press, 1984.

Gray, Robert. *Cougar.* New York: Grosset & Dunlap, 1972.

Grzimek, Bernhard, ed. *Grzimek's Animal Life Encyclopedia.* New York: Van Nostrand Reinhold Company, 1975.

Hallowell, Christopher. "Keeping Mother Nature in Her Place." *Wildlife Conservation,* 96 (1), 1993: 68–69.

Hancock, Lyn. *Love Affair with a Cougar.* Toronto: Doubleday, 1978.

———. *Looking for the Wild.* Toronto: Doubleday, 1986.

Hansen, Kevin. *Cougar: The American Lion.* Flagstaff, AZ: Northland Publishing, 1992.

Hibben, Frank C. "A Preliminary Study of the Mountain Lion (*Felis oregonensis* spp.)." *University of New Mexico Bulletin.* Biology Series, 5(3), 1937:1–59.

Hillard, Darla. *Vanishing Tracks.* New York: William Morrow and Company, Inc., 1989.

Hornocker, Maurice G. "An Analysis of Mountain Lion Predation Upon Mule Deer and Elk in the Idaho Primitive Area." Wildlife Monograph No. 21. Washington, D.C.: The Wildlife Society, 1970.

———. "Learning to Live with Mountain Lions." *National Geographic,* 182 (1), 1992: 52–65.

Houk, Rose. *Great Smoky Mountains: A Natural History Guide.* Boston: Houghton Mifflin Company, 1993.

Hummel, Monte, and Sherry Pettigrew. *Wild Hunters: Predators in Peril.* Toronto: World Wildlife Fund and Key Porter Books, 1991.

Huyghe, Patrick. "Maine Event." *Audubon,* 96 (3), 1994: 18–19.

Jackson, Peter. *Tigers.* London: Quintet Publishing, Ltd., 1990.

Jalkotzy, Martin, and Orval Pall. "The Secret Lives of Cougars." *Nature Canada,* 17 (2), 1988: 21–27.

——— and Ian Ross. "Sheep River Cougar Study Shows Much about Animals." *Eagleview Post,* March 15, 1988: 14.

———, Ian Ross, and J. R. Gunson. *Management Plan for Cougars in Alberta.* Alberta Department of Forestry, Lands, and Wildlife, Fish and Wildlife Division, 1992. 91 pp.

Krebs, John W., Tara W. Strine, and James E. Childs. "Rabies Surveillance in the United States during 1992." *Journal of the American Veterinary Medical Association,* 203 (12), 1993: 1718–1731.

Kunelius, Rick. *Animals of the Rockies.* Banff, Alberta: Altitude Publishing, Ltd., 1983.

Lawrence, R. D. *The Ghost Walker*. Toronto: Holt, Rinehart & Winston, 1983.

————. "Is the Eastern Cougar Making a Comeback?" *Canadian Geographic,* 109 (4), 1989: 32–33.

————. *The White Puma*. Toronto: Stoddart Publishing Company, Ltd., 1990.

Lindzey, Frederick. "Mountain Lion." In Novak, M., J. A. Baker, M. E. Obbard, and B. Malloch, eds., *Wild Furbearer Management and Conservation in North America*. Toronto: Ontario Ministry of Natural Resources, 1987: 656–668.

Linn, Amy. "Wild Cats Wild." *Audubon,* 95 (4), 1993: 22–25.

Long, Tony. *Mountain Animals*. New York: Harper & Row, Publishers, 1973.

Lopez, Barry. *Of Wolves and Men*. New York: Charles Scribner's Sons, 1978.

Lynch, Wayne. "The Elusive Cougar." *Canadian Geographic,* 109 (4), 1989: 25–31.

Mason, Jim. "Going, Going, Gone!" *Audubon,* 95 (4), 1993: 76–83.

Masterman, Bruce. "Turner Valley Rancher Forced to Shoot Cougar." *Calgary Herald,* March 23, 1989: B7.

————. "Cougar Study an Obsession for Biologists." *Calgary Herald,* January 7, 1990: D12.

McKie, Robin. "The Traumas of Returning to the Wild." *World,* 1 (126), 1989: 30–35.

McLeod, Carol. "Going, Going, Gone?" *Nature Canada,* 20 (2), 1991: 11–12.

Morris, Desmond. *Catwatching*. London: Jonathan Cape, Ltd., 1986.

Motavalli, Jim. "Big Cats in the Ozarks." *E: The Environmental Magazine,* VI (3), 1995: 14.

Murie, Adolph. *The Wolves of Mount McKinley*. Washington, D.C.: U.S. Government Printing Office, 1944.

Nordness, Vicki. "Pursuing the Wild Cougar." *Wildlife Damage Review,* No. 5 (Fall 1994): 8.

"Other Alaska News." *Wolf!,* XII (1), 1994: 27.

Packer, Craig. "Captives in the Wild." *National Geographic,* 181 (4), 1992: 122–136.

Paul, Gregory S. *Predatory Dinosaurs of the World*. New York: Simon & Schuster, 1988.

Petersen, David. "Ghost of the Mountains." *Backpacker,* 22 (129) 1, 1994: 16–17.

Peterson, Dale. *The Deluge and the Ark*. New York: Avon Books, 1989.

Quammen, David. "Humble Is the Prey." *Outside,* XVII (10), 1992: 126–132, 220–227.

Quigley, Howard B. "Encounters with a Silent Predator." *Natural History,* 103 (12), 1994: 57.

Rabinowitz, Alan. *Jaguar*. New York: Arbor House, 1986.

Radetsky, Peter. "Cat Fight." *Discover,* 13 (7), 1992: 56–63.

Rauber, Paul. "When Nature Turns Nasty." *Sierra,* 78 (6), 1993: 46–52.

Rychnovsky, Ray. "Clawing into Controversy." *Outdoor Life,* 24 (1) 1995: 39–42.

Reader's Digest Illustrated Book of Cats. Montreal: Reader's Digest Association (Canada), Ltd., 1992.

Ross, Ian. "Lions in Winter." *Natural History,* 103 (12), 1994: 52–58.

Russell, Franklin. *The Hunting Animal.* Toronto: McClelland & Stewart, 1983.

Russell, Kenneth R. "Mountain Lion." In *Big Game of North America: Ecology and Management.* Harrisburg, PA: Stackpole Books, 1978.

Sankhala, Kailash. *Tiger!* London: Collins, 1978.

Schaller, George B. *Golden Shadows, Flying Hooves.* New York: Alfred A. Knopf, 1973.

Schueler, Donald G. "Contract Killers." *Sierra,* 78 (6), 1993: 70–76, 97.

Seidensticker, John. "Mountain Lions Don't Stalk People. True or False?" *Smithsonian,* 22 (11), 1992: 113–122.

Tennesen, Michael. "Ruler of the Canyons." *Wildlife Conservation,* 95 (6), 1992: 38–42.

Thielen, Benedict. "Florida Rides a Space-Age Boom." *National Geographic,* 124 (6), 1963: 858–903.

Thomas, Elizabeth Marshall. *The Tribe of Tiger.* New York: Simon & Schuster, 1994.

Thorndike, Joseph J., Jr. *Discovery of Lost Worlds.* New York: American Heritage Publishing Co., Inc., 1979.

Turbak, Gary. "On the Trail of Canada's Biggest Cat." *Reader's Digest,* 129 (771), 1986: 72–76.

———. *America's Great Cats.* Flagstaff, AZ: Northland Publishing, 1986.

———. "The Cougar Makes a Comeback." *Field & Stream,* XCV (9), 1991: 34–35, 74.

———. "Bounce-back Bobcat." *Wildlife Conservation,* 97 (6), 1994: 22–31.

U.S. Fish and Wildlife Service. *Florida Panther Recovery Plan.* Washington, D.C., 1981. 32 pp.

———. *Eastern Cougar Recovery Plan.* Atlanta, 1982. 17 pp.

———. *Florida Panther Revised Recovery Plan.* Atlanta, 1987. 75 pp.

van Zyll de Jong, C. G., and E. van Ingen. *Status Report on the Eastern Cougar* (Felis concolor cougar) *in Canada.* Committee on the Status of Endangered Wildlife in Canada, 1978. 25 pp.

Voelker, William. *The Natural History of Living Mammals.* Medford, NJ: Plexus Publishing, Inc., 1986.

Ward, Fred. "The Imperiled Everglades." *National Geographic,* 141 (1), 1972: 1–27.

Ward, Geoffrey C. "Enemy and Ally." *World,* 1 (28), 1989: 38–46.

Watt, Melanie. *Jaguar Woman*. Toronto: Key Porter Books, 1989.

"When Wolves and Cougars Meet." *Wolf News,* 8 (3), 1990: 6.

Williams, Ted. "The Lion's Silent Return." *Audubon,* 96 (6), 1994: 28–35.

"Wolves and Cougars: Natural Enemies?" *Wolf!,* 12 (1), 1994: 29.

The Wonders of Wildlife in America. Waukesha, WI: Outdoor World Magazine/ Country Beautiful Corp., 1973.

Wood, Daniel. "Can Cougars Contract AIDS?" *Canadian Geographic*, 114 (1), 1994: 10–11.

INDEX

▼▼▼